Woman Poet

Woman Poet

WOMEN-IN-LITERATURE, INCORPORATED

P.O. Box 12668, Reno, Nevada 89510

Reno/Regional Editions   1980

Cover photo of Madeline DeFrees by Dan Hillen.

Acknowledgment: An earlier version of Tess Gallagher's "Painted Steps" appeared in *Portable Kisses* (Sea Pen Press).

Library of Congress Catalog Card Number: 79-55988
International Standard Book Number: 0-935634-00-2 (paper)
0-935634-01-0 (hardcover)
International Standard Serial Number: 0195-6183

Manufactured in the United States of America

FIRST EDITION

This publication was helped by grants from the National Endowment for the Arts through the Nevada State Council on the Arts and the Coordinating Council of Literary Magazines. We thank them for their support.

Credits for the following photos appearing in the text: Pamela Pavlovsky, page 10, by Richard S. Mayer; Josephine Miles, 14, by Imogen Cunningham; Rosalie Moore, 25, by Sydney Rachel Goldstein; Rita Garitano, 31, by LaVerne Clark; Mary Barnard, 34, by Reed College; Madeline DeFrees, 38, by Dan Hillen; Kathleen Fraser, 51, by Thomas Victor; Adrianne Marcus, 57, by John Poppy; Sheila Nickerson, 61, by Gordon Smith; Mary Crow, 64, by Layle Silbert; Adrien Stoutenburg, 67, by Margo Wardlow; Ann Stanford, 76, by Amanda Blanco; Tess Gallagher, 96, by Hugh Rogers.

Woman Poet

Editor in Chief	Elaine Dallman
Poetry Editor	Carolyn Kizer
Interviews and Reviews Editor	Barbara Gelpi
Special Editorial Advisors	Barbara Mello
	Catharine Stimpson
	Shirley Owen Taft
Librarian Editor	Pamela Pavlovsky
Editorial Board	Susan Baker
	Lois Carrier
	Anne Howard
	Dorothy Kline
	Earline Mason Reid
	Ann Ronald
	Shirley Sousa
Editorial Assistant	Virginia Kristensen
Marketing/Distribution	Cindy Finley
	Marcia Freedman (Israel)
	Pat Morrison
	Lois A. Overton
	Patricia Swaim
	Frances Walker
	Woman unLtd (United Kingdom)
	Stella Savage Zamvil

Editorial Correspondence
Elaine Dallman, *Woman Poet*,
P.O. Box 12668, Reno, Nevada 89510.

Submissions
Virginia Kristensen, Editorial Assistant,
P.O. Box 35, Los Gatos, California 95030.

We welcome unsolicited submissions by writers. Work must be original and unpublished in any version. We reserve the right to reprint. Work which would appear simultaneously in our anthology and an author's collection will be considered if crediting of *Woman Poet* is possible.

We wish we could read all manuscripts in one day's turnaround. We apologize that we cannot. Please allow a minimum of eight weeks for our volunteer editorial staff to carefully read your manuscript. Delays imply no disrespect for the work submitted but reflect the limitations imposed by too heavy a workload.

If work is to be returned, it must be accompanied by a self-addressed envelope with sufficient postage.

Publisher
Women-in-Literature, Incorporated, a non-profit publisher, P.O. Box 12668, Reno, Nevada 89510.

Subscriptions
Charter subscription rates for 2 years, retroactive to Vol. 1 and consisting of four volumes, U.S.A.: institutions $28.00, individuals $18.00, students $16.00. Other countries add $3.00 to cover postage.

Classroom Discount Rates
Please write for special classroom discount rates. Free teacher's subscription with classroom adoption.

Payment
Nevada residents add 3½% sales tax.

Checks should be payable to *Woman Poet*, P.O. Box 12668, Reno, Nevada 89510.

Advertising Rates
Correspondence about advertising inserts should be addressed to *Woman Poet*, Department A, P.O. Box 12668, Reno, Nevada 89510.

Change of Address
Please notify the press and local postmaster immediately, providing *both* the old and the new address. *Allow 6 weeks for change.* Claims for missing volumes should be made within one month of publication. The publishers will supply missing volumes free only when losses have been sustained in transit and reserve stock will permit.

Woman Poet

VOLUME I

The West

Staff Notes

Elaine Dallman

Elaine Dallman (Editor in Chief), always a westerner (except for a stint in Illinois in the 1970's), lives in Reno. She often teaches at the university level. Presently she is interested in Nevada's developing arts programs, believing poet and community must interact and point out to each other the relationship of poetry to life. Most recently, she received a grant from the Nevada State Council on the Arts to teach a workshop for pre-teens based on concepts she developed while teaching in Nevada's rural Poetry-in-the-Schools program.

Carolyn Kizer (Poetry Editor) was born and raised in the West (Spokane); after detours on the East Coast, where she went to college, and a stay in China, she lived in Seattle, where she founded and edited *Poetry Northwest*. After thirteen years of exile in the East (Washington, D.C., Chapel Hill, College Park), she has returned to the West, she hopes for good. She has published three books of poetry and a prize-winning story (her first), and a fourth book of poems is on the way.

Barbara Charlesworth Gelpi

Barbara Charlesworth Gelpi (Interviews and Reviews Editor) is a lecturer in the English Department at Stanford University, where she teaches courses on both 19th and 20th century women writers. With Albert Gelpi she has edited a critical volume, *Adrienne Rich's Poetry*, for the Norton Critical Editions. They both have essays in the recently issued book *Shakespeare's Sisters*.

Shirley Owen Taft (Special Editorial Advisor) was born in England and became a U.S. citizen in 1962. She has taught at both secondary and college levels (especially in experimental settings), and has spent the last few years writing for, and editing, professional and trade journals, technical reports and manuals, and fund raising proposals in basic education, environmental studies, and earth sciences. She is now the writer/editor for W. A. Wahler & Assoc., Consulting Geotechnical Engineers, in Palo Alto, California.

Pamela Pavlovsky

Pamela Pavlovsky (Librarian Editor) is a librarian and children's story teller as well as a writer. A fluent speaker of French, she has traveled widely in France. Her master's thesis was on the writings of Virginia Woolf. She lives in San Francisco and is working on a children's book.

Susan Baker (Editorial Board) is Assistant Professor in English at the University of Nevada, Reno. She helped initiate, and remains active in, the women's studies program at the university.

Lois Carrier (Editorial Board) spent six years with the University of Washington Press in poetry editing as well as in promotion, public relations and manuscript reviewing. Her own poems are widely published, in many university library reviews and in such journals as *Poet Lore* and *Prism International*. She is co-author of a careers education textbook, *Work: Pathway to Independence* (American Technical Society, 1979).

Anne Howard (Editorial Board) chairs the Women's Studies Board and teaches American literature at the University of Nevada, Reno, where she is Associate Professor. She is a frequent contributor to programs funded by the Nevada Humanities Committee, serving as speaker, moderator and/or evaluator.

Earline Mason Reid (Editorial Board) teaches English composition to foreign students in the University of Nevada, Reno, Intensive English Language Center for the Pacific American Institute.

Ann Ronald (Editorial Board) is Associate Professor of English at the University of Nevada, Reno, and Director of Graduate Studies in English. She is the author of *Zane Grey* (1975) and of several articles about women writers of both the U.S. and England.

Dorothy Kline (Editorial Board) has been a high school teacher of English in Michigan and Missouri, a graduate student in English literature at Southern Illinois University, and a university departmental secretary. Presently residing in Reno, Nevada, she maintains an active interest in women writers and characters in nineteenth-century English fiction.

Virginia Kristensen (Editorial Assistant) has been a legal secretary and an executive secretary in the areas of marketing, engineering and credit. She has worked in Iowa, Illinois and New York. Presently, she is Court Clerk of the U.S. District Bankruptcy Court in San Jose, California.

Marcia Freedman (Marketing/Distribution Representative, Israel) was a member of Israel's *Knesset* for four years: 1974–77. She retired to initiate, establish and direct the first center for battered women in her country. In 1979 she opened Woman's Voice, Israel's first women's bookstore, library and research center, in Haifa. Educated in the U.S.

at Bennington College and City University of New York, she has been in Israel since 1969. She has had a book, essays and papers published—chiefly on the subject of women today.

Pat Morrison (Marketing/Distribution) teaches composition classes, with the rank of lecturer, at the University of Nevada, Reno. She received her master's degree in literature there in summer '79.

Patricia Swaim (Marketing/Distribution) has had a varied career—as researcher, editor, social worker trainee, TV newswriter, radio public affairs director, and realtor—while supporting her interest in writing. For her free-lance work, she has won statewide (Florida) awards.

Frances Walker (Marketing/Distribution, Illinois) has been with the Southern Illinois University Press for many years in a number of capacities, presently as systems planner. Part owner-operator of an artists' store in Carbondale, she has recently begun Patches, a cottage industry for the production of soft articles.

Stella Savage Zamvil (Marketing/Distribution, Palo Alto; Menlo Park; Los Altos) received an M.A. in creative writing from California State University, San Francisco, in 1977. Her poetry has been published in *Women Talking/ Women Listening* (Vols. III & IV) and several other publications. Stories have been published in *The Reed*, *Centripetal*, *World Over* and *The Jewish Digest* among others.

Preface

BY CAROLINE KIZER

This is the first of a planned series of regional anthologies which proposes to publish women poets and to focus each volume on the poets of a particular region. As is natural, we begin with our own: what we loosely call The West. As the venture proceeds, we (and that 'we' includes our readers) will be able to determine whether this is a useful and enlightening policy, and the comments of our friends and contributors are not only welcome but positively solicited.

There is the inevitable drawback that poets who should be included will have been overlooked, and will then have to bide their time until we get 'round to Issaquah and Sonoma once again. However, poets are schooled in patience by the inefficiency or plain overwork of small press editors, and this particular disadvantage may be outweighed by the advantages. One advantage which comes to mind will help to mitigate what that wonderful English poet, Ruth Pitter, refers to in her poem, *The Lost Tribe*:

> How long, how long must I regret?
> I never found my people yet;
> I go about, but cannot find
> The blood-relations of the mind . . . .

And if this is true of an English woman poet, how much truer it is for us—in our huge country, where we may be separated from sympathetic colleagues by thousands of miles, but where—so isolated are most women and many poets—there may be a friendly and supportive voice in the next street, in the next county, or a four-hour drive down the road. And there are letters. We hope that a letters column in this publica-

tion will be an additional means of locating those "blood-relations of the mind." The Woman's Movement has spoken to us of the necessity of finding out *who we are*; finding out *where* we are is an adjunct to this self-exploration.

In the letters we write to each other, I hope that we will discuss not only the pros and cons of an anthology in this place, at this time, devoted wholly to the work of women, but the subject of regionalism as well. My own feelings on this are tentative. Having edited *Poetry Northwest* for a number of years, and having lived in the South for a time, I think I recognize certain regional differences in us. Southern poetry tends to be more parochial—oops! What about Mona Van Duyn, from Missouri? Less parochial you cannot be. But then, is Missouri a Southern state? Problems already.

New Yorkers are apt to be more intellectual, to have more references to exotic places, the opera, chess —but it turns out that most of them seem to have done time at the Iowa Writers' Workshop . . . . And are they more cerebral, witty and learned than those three exemplary poets, Ann Stanford, Madeline DeFrees, and Josephine Miles, whom we feature in this volume? Absolutely not.

The best I can say is that we seem to be divided into "inside writers" and "outside writers." Any writer living in the West, though she puts in just as many hours behind a desk as her city-bound sister, is somehow an "outside writer." The city-induced claustrophobia may focus the mind wonderfully, but the focus is more on the self and less on the world around it. In the West, we still have that sense that the world outside is *big*—big but fragile; dangerous and in danger—and we tend to live, not in contempt or fear of our environment, but in awe of where we are. Even in this qualified conclusion I may be wrong. I count on you to tell me.

Josephine Miles

BERKELEY, CALIFORNIA

Trip

We started from a station in the city,
Rough night, wind blowing rain slantwise
On the train windows.
Outside was the elegance of the station.
Hothouse roses in the areas
Of people saying goodbye,
Good luck.
We were the ones going
Into a tunnel of dark
Crying those going-away blues, going-away blues
In our long black woollen stockings and button
        shoes.
Hail, hail the gang's all here
Sang my father to the mahogany walls.
We were not listening and would not sing
What do we care. But we heard him.
The train pulled out of the station into Halloween
The train pulled into November and the passengers
        between
Pumpkin and pumpkin gave us some good
        scares
To wile away the Halloween blues.
Three days and nights in the vestibules
Between cars, roaring and clashing at the heavy
        doors,
Closer to home than the outside scenes.
Then a little
Five minute flash of home.
El Paso is The Pass, my mother said
But it was rather
A burning deck of people in sombreros
Sitting against the sun. Rejoicing.
Now we could see orange trees, smell orange, that
        was a wonder,
And came through that garden to a narrow track
Of train on sand between mountains
Splitting against their ledges,
Nearly empty
The coaches, ledges, rocking along, seeking
Places to stop, with yellow stations
Under pepperwood, under water tank, under signal
Under sky
Nearly empty but our smoke blew in it.
All the baggage is gathered together, we stand
At the last vestibule, we are saying goodbye,
Good luck.

We pile down, look at the little
Boards of the station, turn away
Back to our black coaches, all of us in a row
In our black woollen stockings in the burning sun
To watch them leave us, pull away one by one
With a great grinding.
And they are gone.
And I see, what do we see, all of us,
Stretching my gasping eyes without air or kindness,
Sandy ranges of an infinite distance
Under a white hot sky under
Infinite distance
Beyond a plain, a sea, a life of sand
Of infinite distance
No place to end. A breadth
Hurtful to any small heart
A scope which beached our debris on its shore
Abandoned, lost from a tide of life.
Extended
Not toward us but away,
But we went to it.
Thirsty we drank its infinite sources
Eyes brimmed with its tears,
A hotelkeeper in pith hat and jodhpurs
Drove our baggage into the Springs, in oasis,
But we had gone farther away.

Why We Are Late

A red light is stuck
At the corner of LeConte and Euclid.
Numbers of people are going in and out of the
        7 Palms Market,
Some sitting with beer at La Vals,
Lots lugging bags to the Laundromat—Open—
A couple thumbing rides up the hill, fog curling in
        over the newsrack,
Low pressures.

You can tell it is about five or six o'clock
And we are coming home from a meeting not bad,
        not good,
Just coming along, and stop at the red light.
Time stands there, we in the midst of it,
The numberless years of our lives.
A late green light later
May let us get home.

Demeanor

Here an establishment, its sunny rooms,
Noon offices and beings, vast competitive
Orders, clashes of temper,
Hope forward, elegant energy
Unfolded and disarmed me,
Sharp irony, defense
Turned to a love so swift it went
In and beyond that world like a free runner
    and found
Bodies of love out of belief.
Love of demeanor, love of that face and form
Just as it moved, seldom as I saw it,
Put back together in my asking frame
A fortune of demeanor shapely and true.

Figure

A poem I keep forgetting to write
Is about the stars
How I see them in their order
Even without the *chair* and *bear* and the *sisters*,
In their astronomic presence of great space,
And how beyond and behind my eyes they are
    moving
Exploding to spirals under extremest pressure.
Having not mathematics, my head
Bursts with anguish of not understanding.

The poem I forget to write is bursting fragments
Of a tortured victim, far from me
In his galaxy of minds bent upon him,
In the oblivion of his headline status
Crumpled and exploding as incomparable
As a star, yet present in its light.
I forget to write.

Fund Raising

When Genêt came with the Panthers
To raise defense funds,
The Truehafts stood him on a ladder before their old clinker-brick fireplace,
The bulky man,
Bursting in French English,
His clenched fist swayed the ladder, his wrath
Leaned into the social press
He smiled at Masao, and spat also,
From his compact smooth density of resources.
Hilliard yelled, and others yelled
Until finally someone picked up a bottle and threw it.
It struck Michael McClure's young daughter
Where she sat on the hearth
And she sobbed, sobbed. Michael, schooled as a flame,
Leaped to the ladder and cried in a whisper,
Victims! Always we have to have victims.
The house faded away.
Down the steps of the porch, into cars,
Nobody there.

Noon

Noon students slid onto the unfolded chairs
In the open square where Aldous Huxley stood.
He said, you will be told by those supposed
Wiser, that reason and intuition

Work together, support each other.
But that is false;
Reason is the great saboteur
Do not believe otherwise.

Two o'clock class: What do I believe?
I believe otherwise.

Readers

Jim thinks
This is an angry text.
The professor asks how does he know
Is he right? Will he profess?
Later today I will ask
Is it an angry text? Does he know my mind?
Over this famous text hovers my shadow.
Slowly it moves, the while in the temperate air
Flails Jim's hand and flails mine,
I am angrier than he.
Sometimes with strength of resistance the teacher

Holds back the visible hands,
There is scarcely time for the lot,
And says listen and wait.
Protecting the text, protecting, then does he know
Jim's anger and mine?

Nadirs

There were the clerks of the zenith and the figures,
There were winter-type clouds over the winter
There were summer-type clouds over the summer
    figures
And to speak to each there was a way, the same.
I went up to the clerk of the nadir and said see me
In noctions of one kind or another
Under a winter sun, and see safely to the zenith
How I welter under a blooming moon.
All is mine, but I like it
By each gesture toward the other or one.
So besit, said the clerks of the nadir
And the zenith as they turned to their own
Accounting of afternoon.
They were busy. How busy were they?
They required waiting in line
For the sun to go down over the eastern figures
And the moon to arise over the western figures
Moving from plane to plane.

Josephine Miles: A Sense of Communion

BY JACQUELINE HOEFER

IN AN EARLY POEM, Josephine Miles describes the poet: "On all these streets the truest traveler." The metaphor is prophetic of her own journey, for it is in the streets of everyday life, the common places, that she finds her poems. She goes there with a traveler's enthusiasm, eager to mingle with the crowd, to see with her own eyes what is going on.

What she reports back is deeply satisfying, often joyous, experience. Except for one period, the decade of the Vietnam War, there are only occasional shadows in Josephine Miles' poetry.

How then does she manage to show us ordinary life in vivid high relief? What is her source of emotional color? There is the wit and energy of the poet, of course. There is also her awareness that the significance of personal observation, of personal life even, has been sharply challenged in our time by the success of abstract thought.

Again and again, she contrasts its impersonality with the richness of direct experience. In poems like "Speed" she tells us what is measurable and significant for her: "the real year into which I was born," where "Autumn succeeds summer and every flower / Lives hastily through the steps of its day." And with equal force, what is not: "Unconscionable to me is the speed of a light year / Which I cannot follow with my mind's eyes / Or hear rushing and rattling with my heart's ear."

In "Premiere" the light show that stirs her imagination is not in the heavens, but from searchlights advertising a movie. The searchlights do in fact play on the sky but only "for sign of show," that is, for the movie. They "ask the stars nothing," "Tell them nothing."

Their function is "for more particular sight below." They are "to wake and start / The after dinner heart," and they do: "There is stir in the driveways and rustle of departing." The closing couplet, free of personal pronouns, opens out to include the reader:

> And sight can almost see, ear hear, at the light's
> core
> Gathering, shining, what the lights are searching
> for.

They are searching, we may infer, for the human crowd, hurrying to a show in which the stars are of their own choosing, indeed, of their own invention.

Elsewhere, as in this poem, nature, the world outside the self, whether it be in the heavens or below, is significant only in relation to direct experience. Water is in itself not wet: "That for the thirst, cloth, shower to discover." (Analysis of Compound) Desert is understood "with the skin," "The dry on the voice, the lightness of feet." (Desert)

There is no feeling of uncertainty in these poems. Josephine Miles is confident of her position. That is why she can write so consistently and with such zest about daily life, her own, the neighbors', the youngsters' down the block.

Her own life is very often a comedy of expectations and small defeats. She would show off her summer cottage "By the resounding sea," and finds the view blocked by a housing project, the sea "off the far corner." (Summer) She goes to the movie, midweek, for the Cadillac drawing: "My ticket was number nine seven two seven one," "Certainly a lucky number and easy to remember." (Midweek) But "O heaven" she loses: "The number called didn't even begin with a nine."

In "Campaign," she sits with her neighbors in a vacant lot on a Berkeley hillside. They are there to hear the nominations and the voting on the poet's

Packard Bell radio, "set up . . . near the stump / Of the old peach tree."

While the voice from the Packard Bell drones, "He was a child of the people and he will be a man of the people," the hillside is astir. Apples ripen around the listeners, beans green on their poles, the cat is "active." A fisherman comes through, stops a moment to listen, and goes on, "leaving no vote behind." Speeches become fervent. The moon rises over the rabbit shed, taking its own time. Finally, in early evening, the patient listeners are rewarded: results from the states and the districts begin to come in.

Surely this is the most neighborly of poems. Toward the end of the poem, and again at the end, the poet asks, "Who are you for?" By this time we have come to understand that this or any campaign should be for the crowd on the hillside.

When Josephine Miles writes about children, she usually steps back to watch. A boy, on a sunny morning, searching "for what, sticks / Cans," finds in the shape of a rusty antpaste spike what he dreads and dearly hopes for: "Says the boy with relish, Poison." (Find)

In "Message," the "pony tails" go the movies, "Into the side aisle seats," "Then out to see the fights in the lobby," "Then out up the aisle," "and damn your dime, that's my dime, / And shove," "Then flock back in again . . . ."

Theirs is surely a triumph of life over art. But the older folks deserve some sympathy. Pushed, pulled, stepped on and stumbled over, they must bear up until, blessed relief, the "usher patrol" takes charge, settles this rowdy, irrepressible, and wholly enviable vitality.

Her tendency is toward celebration, though never beyond the limits of her material. Comedy is the obverse side of her coin. That is why, I think, she manages praise so very well. She expects us to laugh as well as to applaud. Our pretensions, as she puts them to us, are indeed comic. Oedipus, it seems, is merely one of the gang, not so very different from ourselves: "The gang wanted to give Oedipus Rex a going away present. / He had been a good hardworking father and king." (Oedipus)

When her subject involves anguish, she never permits us merely to stare. We are engaged sympathetically. In "Ten Dreamers in a Motel," two fat people in a cabin "Some said . . . / Wouldn't hold us two,"

see hundreds of butterflies outside the window. Their response is delicate, appreciative. We understand that what they see in this luminous, darting world are their own spirits, imprisoned by their actual selves.

Josephine Miles' regard for her subject matter is matched by her skill in showing it off. At a time when many poets have abandoned formal techniques and ornamentation, she has retained the immense advantage of utilizing whatever suits her purpose. Thus, her language, which never relaxes into prose, draws on educated as well as everyday experience. The context of her poems reflects what is truly of her world, the literature of Greece alongside the *Berkeley Daily Gazette*, the voices of Plato and Eliot mingled with the noise of the street. She uses with equal skill both tightly organized closed forms and the fluid phrasing and irregular rhythms of prose conversation. Her choice is determined by the poem itself. It must find its own voice, and almost always, the voice is right.

Only occasionally does she succumb to the temptation of the virtuoso. In "Care," for example, the poet complains "What shall I think of you / That makes me worsen?" then traces in Donnean turns of language the turns of feeling that have created an ugly situation. The poem is skillful but, to my way of thinking, overburdened by abstract manipulations. In her best poems there is an openness of statement that admits her liberal intellect without smothering feeling. In "To Make a Summer," she writes: "Sandy says his high-school daughter / Keeps exclaiming joy, joy." But what does it mean? Josephine Miles gives us her interpretation:

> It's a generality, it takes
> From my heart the sting of the singular, it sets moving
> In the easy early Berkeley air
> What we incommunicably share.

Here she expresses a sense of communion, a sense that pervades her work from the beginning.

But the controversy over the Vietnam War jeopardized our common values. The "easy early Berkeley air" was filled with tear gas. Miles' response was predictable. The brutality of public life became the subject of many of her poems. She writes of the arrogance of this "economy of abundance," of our callousness in accepting the horrors of the Vietnam War.

The poems are direct and harshly critical. We have a responsibility, she tells us, that cannot be passed off when the Defense Department "does the blasting."

Passivity is not the only threat. "Daniel Boone stepped up to a window," with its background of the Kennedy assassination, is surely among the best of such poems. Miles uses the frontier hero to comment on the brutality of individual action. The language is ominously comic. Daniel Boone, she says, "shot his bear," "A Harvard, London, and a South Sea bear / A French, a football bear." "It takes no complicated bomb or plot," she concludes, "To win again us back to wilderness."

But anger is not her characteristic mode. She continues to write, as she always has, about the drama of everyday life. An old man runs his wheelchair down the hospital corridor, hoping desperately "to retrieve / Lost efficiencies in the Stock Paper Company." A friend brings the poet a bag of fortune cookies, "Every impossible / Fortune from here to Mishima. / It was the world." A swimmer "in the surf off Seal Rocks" hollers "Help, help, help," and the family on the beach answers cheerfully, "Hello." But above, a stranger, a cub pilot, seventeen, sees and gets the message.

In these poems, we recognize the themes of age and its pathetic battles, of comic expectations, of the casual act that signifies "the brotherhood of man." They relate, in their fundamental compassion, to all our lives.

In "How I Caught Up in My Reading," the poet gives us a list of her summer reading. She has gone through magazines, novels, science fiction, "Your thesis and Betty's thesis and Clinton's / Thesis," the *Berkeley Daily Gazette*, recipes, pamphlets, letters, "a lot of poems," everything.

Her summer reading is a hodgepodge of personal, domestic, intellectual, and popular matter. Its variety is a joy to her, and reminiscent of her work generally. But it is the poem, the work of art, that sustains her as recipe, pamphlet, and letter cannot:

> Then
> I looked around
> and read one poem
> Again
> Again

It sustains us likewise. As we read her poems, we become aware of "What we incommunicably share." Our lives touch, the poet's, our own, the neighbors' she writes about. It is a significant moment, as profound, I think, as direct experience.

* The poems referred to can be found in two collections: *Poems, 1930–1960*, Indiana University Press (Bloomington, 1960); *To All Appearances*, University of Illinois Press (Urbana, 1974).

JACQUELINE HOEFER is a poet and critic. She has written on such important women writers as Katherine Anne Porter, Kay Boyle, and Jane Bowles. Her poems have appeared in various little magazines, most recently in *The Carleton Miscellany*.

Interview with Josephine Miles

BY NAOMI CLARK

Question: What for you are the sources of poetry?

JM: Sometimes when I hear people say something, hear spoken language or see language written, there's a kind of special energy to it which makes me feel that's something I ought to try to keep hold of. Soon, or maybe a long time after, I try to shape it up a bit as a way of keeping it. There's a source of vitality from people. The sense of meaning in what's being said—that's probably where I contribute something. I pick out particular ironies of character and personality and ways of thinking because to me they're touching, amusing, important.

Question: Do you have a sense of any kind of mystical source?

JM: A poet whom I had not met—a doctor—wrote me, "Men's muses are feminine; is your muse masculine?" I'd never thought of it. It's kind of a Jungian thing, but he put it in terms of a straight figure. I'm sure I never thought of having a muse.

There is a feeling when I start a poem, that I'm not sure how it's going to turn out—no surface, conscious control. About half of my students say they get a vague idea, then start writing it; the other half think it all through in their heads before putting it down. The second kind can't revise, the first can. Sometimes I can revise; sometimes I work it out on paper; sometimes, especially when I was younger, it came almost full-written in my head and then I wrote it down. Often I come close to the end and don't think or say "I don't know how this is supposed to end. Where am I going with this?" yet I don't know what's telling me the answer. It doesn't feel very mystical, but on the other hand it certainly isn't very experiential either. Somewhere in between. It's not so much finding something, but bringing it closer to the surface, into fuller consciousness.

Question: Are any of your poems "What if . . . ?" written to fulfill an exercise you'd given a class? For example, "The Day the Winds."

JM: I'm sure some were, though I can't remember that a really good poem has for me ever come out of my giving students an assignment. That particular poem rose from my sense of actual lack of breath rising out of political pressure. That was a McCarthy poem; I wasn't saying, "What if the winds go underground?" I was saying "The winds have gone underground." We were very oppressed here because of the McCarthy thing; there really was a sense of lack of breath. I suppose it might have been a smoggy time in Berkeley, too. The lack of breath became a figure for a kind of political repression we were feeling very strongly. You're right, except that very often events would press the metaphor forward, rather than vice-versa.

Question: Your life and work are illuminated by many kinds of strength. Were particular persons, writers, experiences, ideas, important in developing those strengths?

JM: That's like the muse problem. A poet at Stanford, Vicki Hearne, gave me an answer which I think is good, however. She said it was community. I like that idea. I think of my first community, my family. My parents were unusually good sources of strength because they were different types and disagreed about everything. That's a source of strength, to see people argue without fighting, always coming to different conclusions but still getting along. I found that very powerful and good. I had a couple of interesting brothers, too, who made life various and interesting, and I always had a friend I was fond of. No, maybe one year in three I didn't, and then I was quite lonesome. I didn't have much chance for friends in grammar school because I was in a cast a lot of the time; but even then there was a little neighbor who would come up. We would practice to be opera singers together and that was great. From high school on, in college, in Los Angeles and Berkeley, I have had a sense of sustaining force from the people around me. We have, I think, an exceptional English department here, where everybody in it, I feel, is a source of strength. Then neighbors, helpers—I've relied on student help to take me to class ever since I was a freshman at UCLA 50 years ago, and I've never been late. That's simply astounding—we used to go through tear gas and other thicks and thins up here, but the students have always been dependable. That's a really physical answer to your question.

Question: They must at times have laid down their signs to come to get you.

JM: Yes, they've come absolutely dripping, bloody but unbowed.

If you're speaking of strength in a less personal way, the poet who has meant the most to me would be Yeats, for his sound especially. And over the longest span of time. But one of my sources of strength is that I don't like poetry very well. I love to read it, to teach it, to think about it, but I don't fall in love with many poems. I have a little cluster of poems I've taken out of magazines and kept over the years—probably not more than a dozen, and some I've outgrown. Such a feeling absents me from felicity in a big way; on the other hand, it gives me a chance to do a lot of reading without being touched or terribly influenced. I can even be a fairly helpful critic because I don't take on a poem in any very personal way.

Question: I starred poem after poem in *Local Measures*, a book in which the sense of the importance of local action and of some kind of force holding people together on a local basis was very strong. You didn't get lost in the world.

JM: Yes, I have a sense of the power of the immediate and of the group. I work very hard in each of my classes to get them to become a group. I don't quite know how, and sometimes I haven't been able to do it; but the best classes work very hard to help each other out. Once in a while, we get crazy, violent students, and often they do take poetry classes. It's a marvel to see how a good group can handle—and help—a person who's off the track. Or even on the track. There were three young girls named Barbara in class once who were, I have a feeling, the ones who started Jack Spicer off on his career. He didn't know where he was going, and they were just wonderful at steering him, having a sense of taste and direction to praise him by. Jack was a dominant personality, yet the whole class was sort of making him a poet. That kind of thing happens many times.

I've always wanted to write a really good poem about committee work. I can't do it, and that makes me angry. When a good bunch of people gets together to work on a problem, their minds turning over, responding to each other, meeting the difficulties, shifting positions in terms of what others have said, that's community. I've been on a number of committees at Berkeley that had that quality. Many of my friends laugh at me because I like it so much, but some others on those committees with me agree it's exhilarating. So—families, a neighborhood—I like the whole idea of community.

Question: What do you think is particularly important right now for young poets, women poets?

JM: We need to teach listening, to teach an honest responsiveness. The sense of the other person is part of seeking one's own identity, and I keep asking: "What is one's own identity in dis-relation to anybody else?" Listening is a practice you can give to students. You'd give it to them even teaching political science, history, sculpture. Today's young people need to see themselves in relation to other people. Everybody's been trying to get them to see relations, yet somehow it has resulted in a kind of dis-relation. Isolation and trembling egos puzzle me.

I understand this egocentricity more, more in women, however, than I did before. A first I felt that if women would only just get out and write and quite worrying about it, they'd be okay. But I have learned, working in a campus community, that there are real oppressions, suppressions, repressions, lots of difficulties. One that's very impressive to me, for instance, is that junior high advisors tell girls not to take mathematics past geometry—a simple piece of advice, and a sheer assassination. Yet teachers all over the country, women mostly, have done it. That kind of fact depresses me. But I'm not sure of its relation to poetry.

Still, a little self-confidence goes a long way, and as we learn to sustain women, we reduce, for example, the 40% dropout rate of women from graduate school—40% more than men—to nothing. There are now no more women dropouts than men. That took only two years; we worked, had meetings, talked, reminded women that they were just who they were, and gave them a chance to complain and talk.

The younger women I've worked with around here—Kathleen Fraser, Diana Ó Hehir, Chana Bloch, Sue Griffin, J. J. Wilson, you, all the women in the Comp. Lit. Department who are doing translations, Julie Vinograd, Lynn Strongin, Margaret Casa, Vicki Hearne, Diane Wakoski, Suzanne Juhasz—back to Janet Lewis, Hildegarde Flanner and Rosalie Moore—look what variety. My ex-perience doesn't give me any generalizations about women poets. Look how different they are. That's great, but it doesn't provide a community. I've never yet seen a women's community in poetry, and I'm not sure it's possible or good.

I've tended to stress diversity. I really do have a strong sense of the diversity of everything—tremendous diversity which sometimes comes together in interesting, cohesive ways. That's the good part of life when it does, but I want to keep stressing diversity. The more variety, the more people disagree, the more different ways there are of doing things, the more limitations each person faces in terms of his strength, the more chance there is that when cohesiveness develops it will be a good one because it will be hard won and complex.

NAOMI CLARK teaches English and Women's Studies at California State University, San Jose, where she served as Coordinator for both the Bicentennial Poetry Celebration and the following year's Campus-Community Poetry Festival. These were two of the finest poetry festivals ever held. Clark is the author of the poetry book *Burglaries and Celebrations* (Oyez Press).

Josephine Miles: Narrative Biography

Josephine Miles has been deeply involved in literary activities both nationally and in the local community over the years since 1933 when she came to Berkeley for graduate study. Since 1940, when she joined the University of California faculty, she has combined teaching with poetry writing and research into the language of poetry; she has lectured widely and served as judge in many prestigious poetry competitions. In 1976 she gave the Faculty Research Lecture on the language of poetry. Five of her critical works deal with poetic theory, and she is also the editor of several text books. In recent years she helped establish the Berkeley Women's Center.

Over the years she has also given encouragement to many young poets, perhaps remembering the help and support she herself was given in the 30's by Ann Winslow. Winslow sent Miles' poetry to *Poetry*, *The Saturday Review*, *Scribner's* and *New Republic* and it was accepted. This first major recognition came while she was in graduate school. Also, Ann Winslow organized an anthology of younger poets, *Trial Balances*, in 1935, and Josephine Miles' poems from that collection won The Shelley Award.

Josephine Miles and her family came to California
from the East and settled there when it became evi-
dent that Miles' rheumatoid arthritis was intensifying
and permanent. She grew up with the 20th century
in California, living for a time in the *village* of Palm
Springs, attending Los Angeles High School "out in
the fields of the Wilshire district" and U.C.L.A. "out
in the fields of Westwood." At Berkeley she studied
with James Caldwell and Ben Lehman.

She had written poems, plays, songs and essays as a
child. *Poems Every Child Should Know*, *St. Nicholas*
magazine and *The Bookman* were strong influences
on her as a child by her own claim. She first sent
poems to Harriet Monroe about 1929 and some were
accepted about 1935.

In her career she has been aided by such grants

as the Guggenheim, American Association of Univer-
sity Women, American Council of Learned Societies,
American Academy of Arts and Sciences, National
Institute of Arts and Letters, National Endowment
for the Arts, as well as by the Lowell Award for
literary scholarship from the Modern Language Asso-
ciation.

She retired from being University Professor of the
University of California in 1978. That same year she
added the fellowship of the Academy of American
Poets to her long list of honors.

The latest of her nine books of poetry are *Poems
1930–1960* (Indiana University), *Kinds of Affection*
(Wesleyan), *Fields of Learning* (Oyez), *To All Ap-
pearances*, (University of Illinois Press, 1974), and
Coming to Terms (University of Illinois Press), due
out in 1980.

Rosalie Moore

LARKSPUR, CALIFORNIA

The Phone

Stay with my work.
I decided not to answer;
Its bells unroll a meadow,
The seductive green.

Then it rang.
An exciting silver;
I would not connect with life
Unless I chased it.

The other side of the experience
Undid me: monotonous voice,
Box within boxes of excuses,
Much feeling sorry.

She could not come on Wednesday
She said, but kept on coming . . .
Trudging a road to me, a road
To China, with endless women
Slaving over ironing,
The steaming backs of shirts,
The stretching sleeves . . .

And how escape the words,
The many deaths? . . .
And how does one again
Imagine green?

Near Cologne: 1212

The powerfully confused,
        the Leaders.
Without vision themselves,

they pray for visions . . .
Turning the Morning Star
        by looking at it:
A sense of prophecy swells.

Children walking in white
Carry God on their faces,
Perform what the Great imagine.

Parents with impotent hearts
Turn from the windows
Mourning like sacks.

Any real child
Makes roads actual,
Food granular, odors accountable.

A girl with a simple face
Not stretched to the furious
        adult features
Is grist for the pilgrimage:
The brass of the sun on her cheeks,
The lamb-of-God eyes.

A sounding door flings open.
"Come here" says a voice not magic,
Persuades the child to remain . . .
One phantom less.

Others proceed without thought
Wearing the perfection like a scar,
Moving like short saints forward—
The dolls, the crosses, the bundles.

An old woman runs behind them
Lugging her unsucked bosom;

25

She who no longer has issue
Hates, as a pock-mark, the children.
Throws them obscenities instead of rocks.
No longer mother, she becomes
Their gargoyle fear, their evil dream.

Possessing no one,
She comforts the ugliest women:

Clotilde the clot, the rambling cheese,
The everywhere; her swagger sweet
As pudding, boys to embroil;
Her secret running sore and her
          naked face.
It's the loathsome sufferance
That she detests.
Be not suprised she is evil.

A Baroness distant in the observer's arch:
"We are moving the peasants' children . . .
Faces of clocks,
Rears like mandolins,
And their folkways comic.
I thank you my Lord that you lend them
Such Crusade, for it rids us
Of appetites and the breeding of crimes."

The Bishop, her lover,
Lord of the cleric's castle,
The pewter hurting his hands

As he grips his porridge:
"Rids us of children.
And now are left ourselves.

Face me with stone, O Angel—
And for a relic,
A scald of coals to count
For each child and cherub.

If Jesus cannot save them,
Hell swill me down."

Peeling an orange is reserved for people
In warm, appreciative climates.

Wind at Cologne, the carols
Raged above their heads
And Time seemed doubly to glisten.

In the distinct Alps—
By then, the pain turned into shine
So the pain would be bearable,
The placards of ice
Protecting the different joints.

They thought of love, for stillness,
And fair halls,
And took on their dying
Like an ache of bees.

Diana Ó Hehir

OAKLAND, CALIFORNIA

Alicia's Dream: Entering Knossos

Here's the gate from the sea. The top of it curves.
On one side a lion rests his head on his paws.

Behind him the green holds
White geometric waves; it leads
To a tan horizon, a plume of smoke.

But who's the man with the peacock green eyes; why
Is his hair a pale smooth cap; why
Are the colors of his air as clear
As a painting high up under the clerestory?

Each of us has a new body, I admire your amber skin.
I take your hand, as small as an elegant child's.

The gate of our city is covered in gold.
They'll welcome us home now
On a path like the high causeway
That our ancestors used to walk on, scattering treasure.

Casualty in Mexico City

Our argument echoed down the steps of our hotel, soaked into the carpet.
It had in it glass, coins, the bent remains of a ring,
Tickets for a railroad, and promises, promises,
And the whole week pulled together in a newsreel of gestures,
Faces and mouths and hands,
And you lying on your bed, staring like drowned Jesus at the carved ceiling.

While outside our windows the morning bus to Taxco piled up its logjam of honking cars.
Speak to me, I said to you. The vacancy piled up in our room,
Framed inward by noise,

Brakes squealed, horns honked, the knife sharpener's bell marked time,
The crash of glass became our only way of touching.

Go to the museum alone, I said.
You lay on your bed like a professional crash victim,
Gasped at the ceiling, chewed on your lower lip.

In each of our separate accidents our hands shook for each other.
Our eyes glazed over with shock.

Breaking the Lid of Night

They buried me in gold, stopped up my mouth in copper,
Coated my chest with a turquoise bird,
Swaddled my sex in a pouch of metal,
Poured over that the lid of night,
Perfectly fitting, not heavy enough.

My bones kept saying: wake me;
Knit me back together again; slice off the tattered cloth;
Unclench my arms, stretch each one out;
The leather of flesh will fill itself up with life,
And the light from the open door,
Fierce as claws, rake memory over the brain.

The knot in my throat craves speech; the tongue bends for
A taste of basil, the eyes for
Red light with spinning candle margins, the rusty lungs echo out:
I'm alive! Everything is still possible.

Inside my cupboard of gold a bee is trapped, chilled, somnolent,
Its wings lightly poised over its back.

Olga Broumas

MOSCOW, IDAHO

From: *Of Fruit Whose Black Seed Fire*

1. DEJA VU

In New York we took one day to gawk
breeze-blown from the ferry out
Staten, Riker's island, torch
lit woman striding off
the prison grounds
alone. March
air cold

and sooty but still air
slapping our cheeks and water
grey and greasy but still ocean
water took us in. We giggled
giddy from the inland
drive. We laughed

till Bloomingdale's a black
thin woman, face a blade
of glass, shot
goosebumps through the air, eyes
shut against the showplate, singing.
Summertime . . . We saw her

snap back open switchblade live
inlaid with anger, flat-faced
coins on her plate, then sway
back to the manikins, eyes
shut, another
song. I'm tired

suddenly you said. We didn't
stop. Some jukebox
band in Boston, lovesongs

in a Detroit bar, flat country
western east of Denver, drab back-up
days, no radio, no music
in the car.

2. FOOLS

You feed and feed and feed
me like a fool I eat until
exhaustedly I strike that
spoon out of your hand. What
you wanted: love to lose
the tool your father leaves
you chests
of cutlery and spoons. He lives
and dies and lives. You cry I *need*
you eat and fool I do
not strike it from your fingers—earlier
on so otherwise engaged. White spoons
soft spoons. Beneath them
now in their velvet bed
a regiment of forks grows bolder
rubbing like greedy burghers their
spiky tines. Beneath those knives
big serving scoops
to cup a spleen or liver.
Goldentongued carved-out they clap
each other like a braggart's hand
on his itchy mouth. Let
go now. Burn it. Crush
the smoulders down and douse
that fire. No more love no more
fools spooning up the river
mud. So cool
the open water by us
moves so soon.

3. BREAKING CAMP

Oh not again this coupled
hump, lump, bundle of love
ringed with conditionals, iron lung
with a fickle plug, white porcelain
life-support on *low*. The ice

cubes of my mind, crystalline
babies in twin rows, bicameral, are
melting. Lenses fall like snow. We glow
in the denatured rain, breasts blurring victory
remorse. Born-blind and vicious

intuition cruising
the sewer systems below, an electrode
alert to current, slippery flow
of facts like rats
or moneybags in beet-juice, downstream
from the cannery heart. We have the goods

on each other cold. Rookie cops
on the radarscope, new tickets itching
at our toes. Riot-control, espionage, cold
war. We rise and fall. Still breathing
shocked by the body to the warm

subcontinent, unbarbed, its small
aborigines lacking signals for
weapon, *enemy*, *mine*. Babe, if I have to

push myself off the platform of the crib
wake up in terror falling, alone in walkabout
with bitten nails to break this
dream, I will. I will

not fight with ritual drum, the breath-
tight chant, the vital data cleared by hand, by
heart, by mirror image in the visceral
jungles, safehouse of the gut.

4. SEPARATION

You leave in anger,
confusion, love
struggling between like a blind
woman, feeling
her braille instructions in freezing
winter, cold, with a gloved hand.
I wait for the familiar grief.
A simple pining

not without pleasure, a
lover's angina, sweetly
around the heart.

I slip
into my life without you like a woman slips
back into size nine having
been pregnant only
four or five
months. The clothes
fit. I see her
standing beside a window
leaning against the pane in what seems
like winter, her
fingers that zipped
that buttoned her
into these worn and familiar clothes
returning like somnambules
like inexperienced burglars
to the scene, to the empty crime.

5. LAMENT

Don't
go.

We've shored
up, foreigners
in an inhospitable country
and if our tongue is still
strange in our mouth
our ears, still we know by *bread*
the same gutting hunger, by
heart the same
fiery vacuum sucking
us cold, clean, inside
out:
        the brain
peeled of its membrane
like a glans its perishable skin, the clit bereft
of her ancestral helmet, the eye
lids stripped, the teeth uprooted,
ribcage picked clean, exposing
its fragile scaffold like
a chapel of salt and Oh
the heart
on the open-air altar, beating
for her bowl of human
and feminine
blood.

Rita Garitano

TUCSON, ARIZONA

Morning at Salt River Day School

The teacher talks to Pima children.
The room is a robin's egg blue, the high ceilings
a wash of color. This could be a convent in Sicily.
There is the silence of morning after prayers.

The children are seated at tiny tables. Their faces
are brown corn cakes. But their eyes,
their eyes are night alone in a forest.
The tunnel carved by headlights through falling snow
ends in darkness.

She is the driver leaning into the circle of light
to keep the car from veering, from sliding into the bank.
And there is snow on this warm, still morning.
It is soft and silent and she is weary.

She knows the safety of silence, the warmth of sleep.
If she could take the children home, two by two,
on summer afternoons they would lie in bed beside her.
And she would read until she lost her voice,
long after the children drifted into sleep.

Suzanne Juhasz

BOULDER, COLORADO

Shimmering Threads Like Hair

Sometimes she forgets that her oldest daughter is a little girl.
She allows herself to be fooled by that competent smile,
those matter-of-fact gestures.
She believes her daughter to be her smaller self,
having the same successes but without the same fears.
That her daughter has overcome them, merely by living later.
It is as if her daughter has possessed her own experience
by being present in her mother's body, as spirit
before she was literal (curled shell-shaped fetus, listening):
that in being born she has incarnated wisdom as well as innocence.
So that while she understands instinctively her mother's weaknesses,
she is beyond them. A foolish delusion.
Probably dangerous. Certainly powerful.

She knows that she should give her child back to herself,
should exact no claims of identity upon that slender body,
the eyes clear with intelligence, the limbs poised to dance.
Let her grow from child into woman, all to herself.
As in her day-to-day mothering, she does permit.
But in the secret places of her bones, there the bonds
are ceremoniously cultivated: shimmering threads like hair,
wound over and over, and never cut.

These Women at Thirty-Five

these women at thirty-five
have moved into the faces
that were always their own
but their mothers kept them
out of reach, high
on the shelf in the kitchen cabinet
above the good china

with the real gold rims
along with the ammonia, the lye
the other household poisons
while each night their mothers
drew proper faces on their mirrors
as they slept in dainty beds

one woman says, I have to leave him
it's ok but I need to find a place

I always give my daughter the bedroom
and I sleep on the living room couch
I think that's the right way but
why, when I thought I could trust him
I can't ever be sure again
it's not how it was when I came here
bringing all my dishes
my wool blankets, my daughter

another on the phone saying
he hit me and kept on asking
why won't you cry
and I am beating three eggs
with one hand while we talk
I have to make this cake
for dinner guests tonight
the batter now laced with her shame
leaking into the mixing bowl
she says both men want to put her out
like an empty milk bottle, I think
she says, I could get on a plane
but where would I go

another woman after dinner
sitting with me at the table

lighting cigarettes and saying
I kept the world surreal
my laughter tidying everything
sure I like to fuck but
I sleep only four hours a night
I want no one snoring on my pillow
when I wake at 3 am I read
or clean my dresser drawers
suddenly there is this man
I want to buy new sheets
and watch him while he shaves
but I don't want this to happen

all day I've watched their faces
the bones curving accurately
from creases edging their eyes
the hair growing thick
with need to be alive and moving
and I've thought how
it isn't enough
as I wash the dishes later
place them high in the cupboard
I wonder what can I give them
for the pain

Mary Barnard

VANCOUVER, WASHINGTON

Real Estate

In late May the grasses
are so tall their plumy
waving tops conceal
a sign saying FOR SALE

by Whitfield Bros. The fields
that lately pastured mules
have now become "homesites"
with "riverviews" but still

are rich in clover, lupine,
vetch—rank flowering weeds
fragrant and peaceful, rustling
above wires laid underground.

Journey

Morning:
       a silent singing, a vibration
over the trickling dawn music of creek water
as earth tilts ripple and pool eastward,
awakes in air
stirred yet quiet, tense with shadow
stretched through the valley until the sun
rising crumbles the mountain rim in flame.

For joy of it, water sparkles,
fire pales, bridge planks and grass are warm.
Sun up to sun down, sun up to

Afternoon:
       let water weave on some snow-slope
an umbrella of cloud, a screen of itself, for

itself, of rain. The sun licking the stream
splashes scalding light into shade, invades
the under surface of bridge and leaf
and shrivels water at root source and stem.

Heat pants from the rocks while earth
embraced in the sun's tyranny
tilts downward, eastward, away, toward

Evening:
       heat lingers. Air is tepid.
Darkness comes so slowly even in these deep canyons;
but night falls and the water's own breath,
cool, rises now,
rises towards the mountain walls
bare to the hidden moon, white
with moonlight. Far moon, cold light, memory

moving across the mountain's face,
pantomiming dawn-to-twilight
journeys from twilight till dawn.

Static

I wanted to hear
Sappho's laughter
and the speech of
her stringed shell

What I heard was
whiskered mumble-
ment of grammarians:

Greek pterodactyls
and Victorian dodos

The Gorge

Light has the dull luster of pewter
and the clouds move sidewise clawing
the tops of the crags,
resting their soft gray bellies
briefly in high valleys.

Foam, plowing against the rapids,
gathers all brightness.

The Rock of Levkas

You with the salt-blue eyes
and a storm quivering under young ribs
sea-marked for coral:

You shrieked Fool! when she leapt,
her rigid feet taking the depth of the green
kelp-cloaked surge under the rocks.

The sea wallows in valleys deeper than these;
between remote continents it spins and knots
webs that will snare its rabbit in desert canyons.

Leave the sea coast, leave the river
hollowing its way to the sea.

Find your way into the pines and
higher than they grow, out upon glaciers—
you will not have escaped. Snow
will be whiter than foam between your lips,
tasteless, more quiet, and colder.

The Pump

In the painted quiet
of snow ridges
above peacock rivers
and blond grass scant
over ledges of rock

a pump is quietly
companionable, beating
under the hollow ribs
of untenanted canyons,

unseen, working
to what purpose?

The little slingshot
of sound challenges
an invulnerable silence.

Sandra Gilbert

BERKELEY, CALIFORNIA

Winterpoem

Today is the third Sunday
since the equinox.
My children dance in a froth of ice

at the sea's edge.
All that exuberance of death!
And December,

death's double agent,
tiptoes toward us, whispering
time to go home

(scalpels of frost prying apart the buttery
layers of warmth last summer built,
ice in the veins of the sea, slow

mists drifting toward dark mornings),
time to go back to town
(the gnats doing their death dance above

yellow toadstools just sprung up,
the cypresses drawing inward,
fixing their silence

on the heat behind the bark).
In the city
it really will be

winter:
     shops lit early,
buses coughing down the avenues.

As night falls we'll walk
more quickly from place to place

under misty, motionless skies,

clinging like children to the cold hand
of December, the tough
skin, the iron thumb.

The Dream Kitchen

Her eyes glowed pale as radium.
She said: "Well, if you're good
I'll let you come into
the dream kitchen . . . ."

I was demure. Plaid skirt,
white anklets, gold barrette,
clasped hands always before me
like the hands of the dead.

She said: "Well?"
and I followed her
through the tall door,
and the dream kitchen

with its pulsing ovens
rose around us like a mountain range,
the dream kitchen held us in fleshy
silence, the dream kitchen

rocked us, stroked us,
streaming with syrups and creams
and soupy hollows.
"Check out the cupboards,"

she said. "Open the drawers.
The place is all yours."

I pulled a throbbing handle: streaks of cutlery.
Another: platters inscribed "I'm yours."

"Remember your manners."
I turned to thank her,

but she was gone:
I was all alone.

My enormous kitchen coughed, trembled,
and began to hum.

The Twelve Dancing Princesses

i

Why am I distracted all day, dreaming of the twelve
princesses, their heavy satin skirts, their swift
flight across dark fields, their slow cold sensual
descent into the lake? All day the twelve princesses
circle my furniture like gulls, crying out in a strange
language, proposing mysterious patterns with their wings.
Below them indecipherable ripples wash over the carpet
like white lies.

At midnight the gates of the lake swing wide: the
princesses enter the halls of water. In that bluegreen
ballroom they dance like minnows, darting among stones,
leaping away from circles of light. Even as I write
these words, each solitary dancer is spinning in the
palace of shadow, spinning through night so deep that
the call of the owl is not heard, and the twelve under-
ground princes, wrapped in sleep, row silently away
across the lake.

ii

I am the scholar of the dark armchair—the crimson
wingchair of 1945, the overstuffed gold-tufted armchair
of 1948, the downy satin chair of 1952, and always the
dark chair beneath, the chair immense as the lap of a grand-
father, the chair in which I sit reading the tale of the
twelve dancing princesses.

Winter. Wind on the fire escape. The hush of snow.
Summer. Shouts in the street. Horns, bells, processions
of cars. I curl myself into the dark armchair. I shape
my body to its shape, I do not lift my eyes.

Miles away, at the edge of the city, the twelve
princesses flee toward the airfield. Night swells the arms
of the chair that holds me. The princesses dance in the
sky like helicopters. Below them the lights of the runway
burn in silence, serious as lines on a map or instructions
in a secret book: severe frontiers, all crossing forbidden.

Madeline DeFrees

MISSOULA, MONTANA

Keeping Up With the Signs

Meadowlarks nesting March to August yield
to summer traffic in the dovetailed grass.
Three clear notes. Do Not Walk in Open Field.

I run the way my feet suggest. Upheld
by ringing turf and larkspur flash, I chase
meadowlarks nesting. March to August yield

sways heavy on the cornstalked land I flailed
to find the spot where larks come less and less.
Three clear notes do not walk. In open field,

runways the wind lays flat, fill up. Revealed
in the natural clutch called happiness:
meadowlarks' nesting march to August yield

in the tilt of wind, rainswell and the cold
mating ground, to bed with the dangerous
three. Clear notes do not walk in open field.

I leave five clues for the field guide whose wild
speculation turns the head. Shells express
meadowlarks' nesting march to august yield.
Three clear notes do not. Walk in open field.

Standing By on the Third Day

Coming late to your bed in sleet-ridden
halflight, the moon
lay on her back in the western sky.
Mountains stood in a ring at the cloud-
covered head, their weight
slung over my waist like a sleeper's leg.

In the flare of twin engines, I count my age
in geologic time. I am too young
to leave. Plunged in the ship's wake
this comet opens a crater underwater
deep as the one inside. Bad weather in Denver,
the fallen stars. I have to get out while I can.

You hid the scar I held like wounded
feet to my lips. Exploring caves
you rounded the last
boulder, laid hands on the slow

rise of my body, giving me back a life
that had been let down.

The drone of circling aircraft takes us home
to the island. Staid rhythms prevail
in northerly wind. It crosses my mind how
under the worn serge of a habit another code must
be broken. Whatever vows we speak
will break over our heads in fire or beat the cove
that gave us momentary shelter:

            We have only
this night and the one behind it.

Lecture Under the Moose

*The glass eyes used by taxidermists are generally
too spherical*
   —*Oxford English Dictionary*, December 31, 1869.

Ritual brought us together under that wide
umbrella: an evening of cold cuts
and transcendental moons. All of us
stuffed in winter coats, filed
stiff-legged, past deans preserved in glass,
some taxidermal dream
of large ruminant mammals.

Over the chairs of mounting local heads—a light
snow on the window side—a pair of logger's tongs
swung perilous. Hooked by an expert
line, the framed trout churned water, went down
without glory. This was a big game story
our eyes held, the terrible
territorial gaze of bull moose.

Where now was the shy vernal lover who minced
the tender shoot, loose tongue stripping
softeyed leaves? He wore the season's rack
like a mitre. A clearing appeared in ground
the herd had trampled. Our leader
did not mind whose aegis he was under, spared
the mirror vision our eyes countered.

Whoever stuffed this head, housed eyes in glass,
chose a sphere too absolute. I write this
on a stone. Three young bucks wander

from the herd, tracking moosecalls once removed.
I follow suit, borne on a far
chinook. The antlered brow grows
wide enough to take in what's been thrown.

The moose stands on his head, lowers a hook
like the stick of a bumbershoot
the poor fish grab with tongs. We blow them
ritual kisses. Great Moose, translated
Mighty Muzzle, bemused by rhetoric
your candelabra mounts a wick for every prong.
Transported in that blaze, we speak in tongues,
tranced eyes and reckless heads
lifted off to interstellar spaces.

Gold Ring Triad

This ragged sunflower face glows from the brush
of her lover's hand, opens a space in air.
Like some privileged
giraffe, she peers over fences of neighboring
yards, head half turned to marauding
birds. Watching days fall
and rise, she looks into the leashed
animal lives next door, the intemperate sun
and a caucus of purple finches
campaigning against the cold. Already a chill

invades the old injury, the crooked knuckle stays
what's left of a double wedding ring
half its original size. Cheerful as Martin of Tours
dividing his cloak with the beggar
my mother took that wide souvenir from her finger
to give me an equal
share. With a narrower band I promised I'd marry
no one, live for everyone
behind the high stone wall: it was
a marriage in air, a bond
sealed until I could breathe

                                    no longer in that zone
high above the clouds. My head quivered,
a severed and perilous freight. To steady the wealth
of my own ground, I had to trespass outside the gate,
play Jack and the Beanstalk. Imagine a squirrel,
sure-footed flagpole saint, sent
up that stem into the closed fist of sky. Briefly,

the rodent sways, raffish head,
death's-head, the ongoing neck: how exposed
the staff that keeps us vertical!

                                    In this replicated
sun I praise everything that fuses clay
and fire: earth broken and tilled,
the usual harrowing
sign of division. And I remember pain, confined
by my portion, waiting in the hospital bed
for the disk to mend. My body
worn so thin the ring slipped from my right hand
and fell unnoticed. At home
I missed that relic of two lives
I could never find again.

                                    And you, my sister, my friend,
knew my grieving, gave me back the dead
woman's share. I wore it on the left, hand of true
marriage, pledge sinister. Relic of unions
blessed though not made in heaven, my poor
lost mother, almost a child bride. In the first
luster of final vows I tried to appear older, rub initials
smooth. Her half, profane
from the start, bore none: no Jesus, Mary, Joseph
to pillow the dying head.

                                    It was destined to take me
elsewhere. I wear that ring in bars, in bed, wherever
it fits, the right little finger
beside the opal that is not my stone: half-lost
ring of my dead mother
forgiven, ring of abandoned lives
knit into my own.

Slow-Motion Elegy for Kathy King

I roll the pebble of this word on my tongue, feel
the sting, the hard
salt taste of it. They never get it straight.
No way to splice the reel of wreck
and exile, the silent
film. You have passed on
to life in that cloudy home, leaving your friends
weighed down, shortening days
without you.

Into the world, into the cloister
and out before me: whatever the future held
you held it first. Two sides of an old oak door
we traded supervision during lunch
and startled high school seniors with our French.
That year the enemy who struck you down
enlarged your heart. How soon these summer
reruns make me sad.

Twelve months in bed and
you were
back mountain-climbing stairs.
To think I envied you the sound track
fading out, the rest.
A walk-on strangler found the fire escape and broke
your dormitory sleep.
You said it was a shortcut
to a private room, the violence you dreamed
locked in by a double door.

I saw it mirrored there.
Left behind, trying to name this
anger, this more-than-morning sickness, I interrogate
the tide. When you were mugged

police said, Do you still believe in civil rights?
A terrible neighborhood: they didn't ask you twice.
I watch you moving in to stay. Your brave words
skipping stones farther out than mine. Now they are
going down, coral and skull to lime.

If I could
match that other orator, the sea, I'd rage
out of bounds, beat the rock
you threatened. Lashed to the mast but never tied
to the script. No child
wearing a halo
ladles the ocean into this hole at my feet. A tourist
stalking elegant cuisine
appears to me. How easily the mind snaps
shut on itself, a razor clam.

How shall I know
the changing women I am: the hermit crab scrawling
a private code. Dolphin, smart and playful,
towing a man-sized brain. The killer whale spouting
news of deep water. Nothing's
the right matter. These waves break over me
and break again.

Domesticating Two Landscapes: The Poetry of Madeline DeFrees

BY M. L. LEWANDOWSKA AND SUSAN BAKER

THE POETRY OF Madeline DeFrees shows the steady but difficult progress toward self realization of a poet. The early poems, gathered in *From the Darkroom* (1964), present predominantly objective, philosophic statements, embodied in simple, direct metaphors and caught in tight, schooled metrical patterns. In her next collection, *When Sky Lets Go* (1978), forms loosen, and her poems become more personally intense as attention shifts from the outer world to an increasingly complex inner one. *Imaginary Ancestors* (1978), DeFrees' latest and most mature work, incorporates tones of prose and narrative into fully poetic, lyric explorations of the past that has created the strong, self-determined persona of the present.

DeFrees' experience as Sister Mary Gilbert in the Congregation of the Sisters of the Holy Names of Jesus and Mary dominates both her first volume of poetry and two prose works, *Springs of Silence* and *Later Thoughts from Springs of Silence*. If we learn from the prose writer what strictures of discipline and self-denial her vocation demanded, we learn from the poet what that constraint cost, how it felt, how it shaped her vision of the world. Her early poetry is not, however, simply or only about life as a nun. On the contrary, DeFrees uses images of convent and habit as Roethke used those of the greenhouse—as metaphors to convey universal emotional states. In this case, the images define an emotional life in conditions that are restrictive, confining, egocrushing.

"Learning to Fly without Latin," one of DeFrees' later prose pieces, reveals much about her early world:

"To live in a Latin universe is to build a cage as intricate as the bird's whose song beats against the bars. In that lyrical past when the horarium really sounded to me like God's voice, I spent my birdlike days in such a prison. Poking the head out at predictable intervals to shrill 'Cuckoo' might give the illusion of freedom, but it did not alter the entrapment in time." The metaphor is apt; in DeFrees' early poems she kept her self within a splendid cage of form. She said much, but she stoppered up more within *From the Darkroom's* meticulously polished verses where every syllable and stress is calculated in even measure and rhymes chime in perfect pattern.

Within these perfectly drawn lines there is a world of hush, of numbness, of objectification. There are, for example, no individuals; there are people, yes, but only nuns in groups, strangers on a bus, two "he's" personifying "criticism" and "poetry," and one "Irish poet." In this world, time is measured not by events, but by the passage of seasons. Sometimes seasonal changes in landscape are abstracted to provide metaphors for a sense of being trapped in time: for example, "A winter stillness settles on the heart" (Frozen Sleep); "frost that kills and cleanses has returned / to burn my thousand wounds to senselessness." (Axis) Other seasonal changes are made concrete: "Planed smooth long before Autumn / the sycamore bares bone to lonely stretches." (Gestures of Autumn) Yet the limitation remains; this is still a generalized landscape.

In "From the Darkroom," the negatively charged context of constraint is reinforced by pervasive images of death, paralysis, or uselessness. In "Recession," for example, we see how "The year's fruit," a "bruised burden," awaits the coming of the "slow frost" which will destroy it while "the heart grows numb." "Skid Row" ends with images of a night when "The bruised reed breaks and the sparrow falls." Or, pointedly, DeFrees shifts the environment to indoors in "Antique Convent Parlor" where "Flowers would only die in the fluted bowl, / sighing for parallel sun through shuttered dark."

Still, pushing against the dark places are poems of sudden joy. Significantly, the celebratory poems most often rejoice in an escape from constraint of some sort. For example, "Whitsunday Office," which responds to the speaker's first hearing of the liturgy in English, begins "Loosened, their tongues take fire," and concludes in an allusion to *Corinthians*: "One glass the less to see through darkly / brings the Image near." "Elemental" expresses the eruption of emotion, emotion that has been contained by enforced discipline:

> Denied the upper air
> Where burning is clean and free,
> Fire sinks below the stair
> And creeps along the floor
> To plunder endlessly.

In the final stanza the fire bursts into overt images of ecstasy, in a Roethkean cadence:

> I waken from the sleep
> Of disciplined desire
> To waterfalls of light
> And pinnacles of fire;
> Survey the flaming north
> The whirling upper air,
> And fling myself to earth
> To take my comfort bare.

Such a poem prepares us for the great move toward freedom recorded in *When Sky Lets Go*, published fourteen years later. From the first poem of this collection we are clearly in another imaginative world, one with strong, sharp images of specific people and with streets and rivers and cities given specific names. Here DeFrees uses a sharply controlled free verse, believing perhaps what she writes in "Paying My Taxes," that "Computer love is like the poetry: / more exciting when routines break down."

In this world, relationships are more personal,

more mundane, as we see at the party described in "The Odd Woman":

> We come to my coat laid out
> . . . . I know
> how a woman who leaves her purse behind
> wants to be seduced. I hang mine
> from the shoulder I cry on.

When Sky Lets Go is divided into three sections. In the first, "Watch for Fallen Rock," the persona explores new territory, makes new contacts, discovers new traps. The dangers of this new life are implied in the title poem of this section; for example, one metaphoric line describes how life now flows "In surprising turns the road signs missed."

The second section, "The Blue Nun," describes the long, most difficult road to freedom. Aware of her own paralysis, the speaker of "Barometer" tells us "all through a cold Spring / it has been snowing somewhere at the back / of my mind." She endures illness, despair: "I fall asleep at the edge of winter / its thin blade at my throat." (Filling in the Report)

When the emotional break comes, it is sudden, joyous, and captured in a psalm's description of a freed bird: "*My life was rescued like a bird from the fowler's snare. / It comes back singing tonight in my loosened hair.*" (Psalm for a New Nun) The last poem in this section, "With a Bottle of Blue Nun to All My Friends," bursts forth unforgettably in wildly exhilarating black humor:

> Sisters,
> The Blue Nun has eloped with one
> of the Christian Brothers. They are living
> in a B&B Motel just out of
> Sacramento.

As she has arranged the final section (Pictures on the Shifting Wall) of *When Sky Lets Go*, the poems perceptively analyze a new condition: "Light from a used sun flooded the street / where I stood, half woman, half nun, exposed." (Existing Light) From this place she explores old wounds, relationships with father and mother, their deaths. She is aware of the double-edged nature of freedom, its terrors and challenges, its trials and joys. This dangerous necessity is summed up in "Domesticating Two Landscapes," the opening poem of the section. The book ends, however, not with the terrors that haunt the explorer, but with the excitement known to the prospector: "The lure, the lore of the hidden. Every side / of refractory matter splitting light. Excited / atoms cooled to latticed arrangement. A deep / blaze waiting to surface." (Hope Diamonds [This is DeFrees' correction of the book])

The promise of these lines is fulfilled in DeFrees' third collection of poems, the chapbook, *Imaginary Ancestors*. These eleven poems, her most recent ones, are DeFrees' finest creations. They explore a poet's roots—biological, religious, creative—and culminate in the confrontation and acceptance of the most intimate realities:

> The body
> meets the animal it ran from: dark bush
> parted in the night, wet fur, the cave lighted
> by the eyes of lynx, my own
> dense longing.
> (The Woman with Fabled Hair)

Such lines suggest the impressive new tone of DeFrees, announced by the title of the first poem in the collection, "Honesty." A new directness, confidence, and simplicity give this group of poems a remarkable accessibility, even as complex themes are explored. For example, the description of the speaker's mother is vivid, concrete, compelling:

> Mother went to school in a cyclone cellar. She
>   learned
> not to fight long-haired cats,
> not to interrupt or make noise, not to lie
> or cry over nothing.
> (The Bishops Bring Tablets of Stone)

The will to know oneself through understanding one's ancestors, to know the present through coming to terms with the past, reverberates through this volume. "Grandmother Grant," for example, records the poet's determination to search for the story of her unknown maternal grandmother, despite discouraging replies to inquires made at the orphanage, despite the possibility that "he knocked her down / in the stinking hold of a ship and raped her," despite the perhaps more threatening possibility that "she followed him out of the church / into the oldest garden." Here, too, the poem ends simply, straightfor-

wardly, "Whoever she was, whatever ties, / here is my claim. I need to come into my own."

This need is fulfilled, surely, in these latest poems. However, it is not sufficient that the poet reclaim her heritage; she must also exorcise aspects of her particular past. Perhaps we see this exorcism in "The Widow." The poem begins by describing a nun, "There was a self-made widow far back in the trees, / wore black even in summer, black / to her unsung bridal." She moves in a world with "Windows of unreal space," this image recalling the abstract landscape of DeFrees' early poems; she is barred from direct experience, having "Never the clear gaze of the whole woman." This description echoes the price of constraint, as suggested in such poems as "Whitsunday Office" and "Elemental." The final stanza of "The Widow" recounts the woman's physical shattering and her concomitant release:

> Today October haze
> crowns the mountain, leaves crack underfoot,
>   shock
> tilting earth's crust. Black glasses I wear
> peer through her eyes as I kick
> the leaves aside and sing for the widow glass.
> She falls at my feet breaking the cold surface,
> ash floating on air the dust settles.

The scene and season are here realized in few, but precise and concrete, images. Such clarity of statement can only be hard won, but this poem and the collection in which it is found celebrate the creation of a vital landscape, one in which a woman and her poetry can thrive.

—*M. L. Lewandowska and Susan Baker*

LOU LEWANDOWSKA, Coordinator of the Creative Arts Program at San Jose State University, is Associate Professor of English there. She is a poet, critic and writer of fiction. Among her 1978 critical essays were ". . . Roethke's Use of the Psalms of David," *The David Myth in Western Literature* (Purdue U. Press), and "Feminism and the Emerging Woman Poet," *Itinerary Seven*.

SUSAN BAKER was one of the initiators of the Women's Studies Program at the University of Nevada, Reno, where she is Assistant Professor in English. She teaches modern and contemporary poetry as well as subjects in Renaissance literature.

Interview with Madeline DeFrees

BY ROSEMARY SULLIVAN

Question: Did you begin writing poetry early and
did you always have the desire to become a writer?

MD: I remember writing my first verse when I was
eleven and in the seventh grade—an assignment for
Mother's Day. From then on, I wrote verses, stud-
ied versification, read anthologies and kept note-
books. All through high school I wrote adolescent
philosophy in rhyme and meter. Next I wrote re-
ligious verse and versified "simplicities," amateur
dramatic presentations with which postulants and
novices entertained one another and the "professed
sisters," those who had already made their vows.
I wrote Hopkins imitations and Dickinson imita-
tions for two or three years. Eventually, I want to
say inevitably, I wrote poems.

At home, my writing was something that gave
me a private place—one Off Limits to my mother
and my younger sister unless I chose to make an
exception. If I thought that either of them had
read one of my poems without permission, I tore
it up.

Question: From the Darkroom was published in
1964 when you were 45. That's late for a first
book. Were you discouraged from writing in the
convent? Or were you frustrated by convent dis-
cipline?

MD: The pace of my publication wasn't too unusual
in that milieu at that time. After all, I began col-
lege in 1936 and received my B.A. in 1948. The
convent horarium left little time for writing, and
we were discouraged from letting our minds wan-
der to such "distractions" during periods prescribed
for mental prayer or those regarded as remote
preparation for it. "Grand Silence," which extend-
ed from 9 p.m. until after Mass the following morn-
ing was such a period. When you exclude hours

given to class preparation and teaching, along with
mealtime spiritual reading, there's not much space
for poems. My own view is that such systematic
exclusion doesn't work: poems and the habit of
mind that generates them refuse to obey schedules.
Suppress them in one place and they pop up in
another. The result is bound to be sleeplessness,
double-vision, and a lot of guilt. Sometimes it's
good for the poetic impulse: it has to be very strong
to force its way through the obstacles.

Then, too, I think I had a fairly realistic view
of publishers' interest in poetry, and when most
were doing only one or two books a year as pres-
tige-builders, I didn't think my chances were very
good. Strangely enough, the Sisters, too, seemed
more impressed by how much money was paid for
a given piece of writing than by the magazine in
which it appeared or the quality of the poem. They
were usually apologetic about this—"I know this
isn't important, but how much . . . ?" So I did little
to pursue book publication until Samuel Hazo
urged me to submit for the YMHA-YWHA contest
in 1962. I was at St. Mary's, Notre Dame, and he
came there for a reading. The judges were Kunitz,
Bogan and Lowell, and my manuscript was a final-
ist. When I mentioned the poems to my editor
at Bobbs-Merrill, indicating that of course he
wouldn't be interested in poetry, he told me to try
them. So far as I remember, the book didn't even
earn back the $500 advance they gave me.

Question: It's a shock to see such a sophisticated
first book as *From the Darkroom*, but perhaps
that's because you had been writing for many years?

MD: As I mentioned earlier, I did a lot of exercises
and reading during the early years. All through the
novitiate I read, memorized and meditated on the

45

poems of Gerard Manley Hopkins. The silence, the introspection and the minimal intrusion of the mass media had certain positive effects. And because I shared my love of poetry with few persons in the Order, I learned to broaden the base by seeking out the visual artists and the musicians. I think that the poems in my first book give evidence of that.

Question: Looking at *From the Darkroom*, what strikes me are the violent and restrictive organic images. For instance, the image of fruit on a blighted tree is obsessive and there is an intense sense of claustrophobia in the poems. If you were trying to camouflage this feeling from the sisterhood, you didn't succeed. What were you trying to camouflage?

MD: Surely it can't come as any surprise to you that the Tree—of the Cross and of the Knowledge of Good and Evil—loomed over that landscape. As for the claustrophobia, I presume that you refer to poems such as "Elemental" and "Where the Light Begins." From my present vantage point, it would appear that *enclosure* magnifies sound in much the same way that a rock falling inside a cave echoes and reverberates. I have come to believe that the entire range of human experience is present in the convent: only the gradations or scale differs. The evasiveness or indirectness or vagueness I now see in those earlier poems stems partly from temperament and early habit (trying to keep things from my mother), partly from the convent ideal of serene composure, which, in my case, intensified the unacknowledged or unacceptable feelings; and, perhaps most of all, from the inability to deal with sexual feeling in a mature way. Gradually, I came to understand that most of the Sisters were unsure in the presence of poems, and, if I could act as though everything were innocuous, it would be.

Question: Between your first and second books, your life changed radically. You left the convent, and of course the experience is recorded in your poems. You speak about nuns as watchers—"witness" is the word you use—and about your eventual dissatisfaction with that position: to be cut off from experience was intolerable. Yet the decision to change must have involved much guilt and confusion.

MD: In a sense, yes, but such changes seldom come about abruptly. I had begun living more or less on my own in Montana from 1967 (when I went to the University to replace Richard Hugo for a year) until 1973, when it became clear to me that my real life lay outside the Order. By that time my mother was dead, and I had learned how to negotiate the "real world" less awkwardly. I had tenure and Social Security, and after the initial trauma of confronting the big decision, what I felt more than anything else was relief.

By that time, too, I had decided on my own that I needed psychiatric help, and as I learned to express anger instead of letting all of it turn to guilt, I trusted my feelings more. Once I began telling a few others about my decision to leave the convent, I experienced a sense of wholeness and peace unprecedented for me. And I began to get all kinds of ideas for short stories, delivered from the image of what was "appropriate" for a nun to write. I became convinced that a subtle self-censorship had been operating for years.

Question: What do you think were the things that held you in the convent? Was your family a powerful influence? Your mother haunts the pages of *When Sky Lets Go.*

MD: Things that held me . . . . Fear, certainly. One story from novitiate days that made a deep impression concerned a postulant whose parents persuaded her to come home. Shortly after, she was killed in an auto accident. That kind of prompt retribution had its hold on me.

Then there was my mother. Because both my brother and my sister had divorced and remarried, I became my mother's proof that she had brought us up right. Now I realize that I may have underestimated her ability to change. My whole effort to repossess my past is a way of refusing to allow it a death grip, not falling into a kind of hopelessness or powerlessness because of it.

Question: In one poem, you write of how "the body meets the animal it ran from." Is it a relief to write love poems?

MD: For a little while—until somebody decides they are about baptism, drowning or big game hunting in the Montana wilderness.

Question: Being a nun, in a sense, means giving up one's femininity: you speak several times of the shaved head of the novice. Does claiming back your authority as a woman lead you to identify with other women who are doing this?

MD: Not once in all my twenty-nine years of wearing the coif and veil did I shave my head! But I knew a few sisters who did. However, I sometimes make that symbolic concession to the reader, and as a symbol it's accurate.

As for the second part of your question, I do feel that my emergence from the cloister gives me a strong bond with women whose lives were superficially very different from mine. I know how that housebound mother, newly divorced, feels when she suddenly has to come to grips with independent living. I know the problems of learning—or re-learning—to drive at fifty, the difficulties of budget and finance, of credit and real estate, machines and repairs, dealing with a society built for couples.

Question: Your early work was very formal. In a sense you were as strongly constricted by linguistic restraint as by the convent walls.

MD: That wasn't too unusual for writers of my generation, and now that I've been teaching for some time I realize that forms often liberate the imagination of beginning writers. The involvement in satisfying the requirements of the form offsets the anxiety and diffidence about succeeding, silences what Gail Godwin calls "The Watcher at the Gates." Too much freedom can be disquieting, and for some time after I left Spokane, I carried the walls with me, though I had pretty well discarded formal writing.

Question: Who are your models now?

MD: This question might be easier for somebody else to tackle because, at this point, "influences" are more likely to be indirect and more thoroughly assimilated. When I am trying to dispose myself for writing, I usually read in unfamiliar areas—say, landscape architecture or an article on precious gems. What is important is to experience language in a fresh way by entering different word worlds.

I do have other kinds of models, however. For sheer staying power (an important quality for us turtles) I turn to those who have retained creative vigor into advanced years: people like Picasso,

Casals, Robert Penn Warren, whose poems show an astonishing growth and resilience. I derive strength from numbers of women who have managed to keep on writing under heavy odds and with minimal support: these trail blazers make it easier for the rest of us. Among the younger women writers, Tess Gallagher is a favorite. I hesitate to acknowledge all my debts because there are so many I'd be sure to leave someone out. But it would be easier to give a history of "influences" than to identify the current ones.

Question: Does the increasing personalization in your work imply a desire to probe more deeply into the area of private experience?

MD: Unless private experience is somehow transformed or transcended, I see little excuse for putting it in a poem. On the other hand, the lyric is, by definition, *personal*.

Question: What changes have occurred in your work?

MD: Some modifications in what I'll call my "dark vision," the kind of preference indicated in "Hope Diamonds." Changes in lining that give the poems a different look on the page. Less frequent use of the ironic tone, some of which has been redirected into fiction. And the absorption with early experience, which seems fairly common with writers at the age I've attained. There's new experience, too, because I have a lot of time to make up for, but the words that come most often to my poems these days are *my own*. After so many years of institutional living and authority hang-ups, I value my privacy more than ever and luxuriate in being able to stand free and clear, accepting myself—most of the time.

In 1974, ROSEMARY SULLIVAN and Doug Beardsley (another young Canadian writer) interviewed DeFrees at Victoria, but the interview was never published. Now Assistant Professor of English at the University of Toronto on leave in England with a Canada Council Grant, Sullivan was glad to help us with an experimental interview. She sent the questions from England, DeFrees sent answers from Montana to *Woman Poet*, editor Gelpi cut/edited.

Madeline DeFrees: Narrative Biography

Madeline DeFrees, third child of Mary (McCoy) and Clarence C. DeFrees, was born November 18, 1919, in Ontario, Oregon. Her parents, deeply affected when the first child, a daughter, died in infancy, became over-protective toward their next children, particularly the son, who was dressed in white for the first years of his life. The mother knew nothing of her own parentage, having been taken at four from the New York Foundling Home to St. Louis for adoption. Perhaps it was the emotional burden of the mother which led to the daughter's need for a separate "self" expressed in the poems she started writing when she was ten.

The family moved to Hillsboro, Oregon, then a town of three thousand, where Madeline began first grade before her fifth birthday. A compulsive reader, she went outdoors to play only when her books were hidden by her mother. "I was a terrible tomboy when I wasn't being a bookworm," she says. "I never liked dolls except for an ugly ragdoll my grandmother made, preferring stilts, rubber guns, and scooters made of apple crates, two-by-fours and old skate wheels."

Her mother refused to send her to public high school, and Madeline resisted attending the academy in Beaverton, nine miles away. They compromised. She lived with her cousins in Portland, Oregon, her freshman year and attended St. Mary's Academy. There she admired the nuns who taught her and hoped to join them later. She entered the novitiate of the Holy Names of Jesus and Mary at Marylhurst shortly after high school graduation.

Her higher education began at Marylhurst College, Oregon. She received a B.A. in English literature, *magna cum laude*, in 1948; then continued at the University of Oregon for an M.A. in Journalism, meanwhile taking further work with Karl Shapiro, Markham Harris, John Berryman, and Robert Fitzgerald. She has taught at almost every grade level, beginning in Oregon elementary schools, moving to private high schools in Oregon, then to Holy Names College, Seattle University, and finally, in 1967, to the University of Montana, where she is a tenured professor of literature. It was after she taught at Montana for six years that she officially withdrew from the Order.

In addition to her regular teaching, she has taught various poetry workshops in the Northwest, has served as a consultant for the National Endowment for the Arts Poetry Grants, the Montana Poetry-in-the-Schools Program, and the Bush Foundation, and served as a faculty member at several Alumni Colleges for the University of Montana.

She is well published in numerous anthologies, and has also published literary criticism on James Wright, Sandra McPherson and others. Her poems have appeared in *Sewanee Review*, *New York Times*, *Saturday Review*, *The New Republic*, *Choice* and in scores of regional and university publications. Among her fiction is one publication in *Best American Short Stories*.

Her two prose books are *Springs of Silence*, an autobiographical account of convent life, and *Later Thoughts from the Springs of Silence*. Her first poetry book, *From the Darkroom* (Bobbs-Merrill), came out under the name Sister Mary Gilbert. Her second and third poetry books, *When Sky Lets Go* (Braziller) and *Imaginary Ancestors* (Cut Bank/Snake Root Press), both came out in 1978.

Joy Harjo

ALBUQUERQUE, NEW MEXICO

The Black Room

She thought she woke up.
Black willow shadows for walls
of her room. Was it sleep?
Or the star-dancer come for her dance?
There are stars who have names, who are
dreams. There are stars who have families
who are music. She thought she woke up.
Felt for skin, for alive and breathing blood
rhythm. For clothes or an earring she forgot to
take off. Could hear only the nerve
at the center of the bone—the gallop
of an elegant horse. She thought she woke
up. Black willow shadows for walls she
was younger then. Her grandmother's house
sloped up from the Illinois River in Oklahoma.
The house in summer motion of shadows   breathed
        in cool
wind before rain rocked her. Storms were always
quick could take you in their violent hard rain
and hail. Gritty shingles of the roof. Rat
rat rat ratting and black willow branches twisting
and moaning and she lay there, the child that she was
in the dark in the motion. She thought she woke up.
Joey had her cornered. Leaned her up against the
wall of her room, in black willow shadows his breath
was shallow and muscled and she couldn't move and
she had no voice no name and she could only wait
until it was over—like violent summer storms
that she had been terrified of. She thought she
woke up. Maybe there were some rhythms that weren't
music. Some signified small and horrible deaths
within her—and she rode them like horses into
star patterns of the northern hemisphere, and
into the west.

This morning she thought she woke up.
Alarm rang and fit into some motion, some voice
within her other being—a dream or
the history of one of the sky's other stars.
Still night in the house. She opens
herself for the dark. Black horses are slow
to let go. She calls them by name but she fears
they won't recognize her, and if the dance
continues in nets of star
patterns
would it be sleep?

Call It Fear

There is this edge where shadows
and bones of some of us walk
                              backwards.
Talk backwards. There is this edge
call it an ocean of fear of the dark. Or
name it with other songs. Under our ribs
our hearts are bloody stars. Shine on
shine on, and horses in their galloping flight
strike the curve of ribs.
                    Heartbeat
and breathe back sharply. Breathe
                              backwards.
There is this edge within me
                    I saw it once
an August Sunday morning when the heat hadn't
left this earth. And Goodluck
sat sleeping next to me in the truck. We had
never broken through the edge of the sing
ing at four a.m. to reach our bodies
        we had only wanted to talk, to hear

any other voice
                    to stay alive with.
                            And there was this edge—
not the drop of sandy rock cliff
bones of volcanic earth into
                            Albuquerque.
Not that,

                    but a string of shadow horses kicking
and pulling me out of my belly,
                    not into the Rio Grande but into the music
barely coming through
                            Sunday church singing
from the radio. Battery worn-down but the voices
talking backwards.

Kathleen Fraser

SAN FRANCISCO, CALIFORNIA

Casuist, Etc.

Casuist, quibbler, jelly-heart, equivocater, hedger, shuffler, beater about
bushes, back-door-enterer, beggar-of-questions, splitter-of-hairs, strainer
at gnats and swallower of camels, caviler, side-stepper, claptrapper, moon-
shiner, sophist, prevaricator, palterer, paralogist, distorter, shifter-of-
feet, evader of issues, I have loved you too well.

Joan Brown, about Her Painting

There is a black dog in my painting.
He says Woof.

You recognize this message, don't you?

It is a gesture
as typical
as the mechanical pleat of laughter.

I have decided to give up my pallette knives
and my "typically vivid" colors. He approved
of me so much

I couldn't hear, so for months I stood
before the canvas   and made tiny strokes
on a "highly irregular" still-life,
still
breaking the pattern of woof and bow-wow.

I loved so much my red and black.

I needed confidence   and the tiny brushes whispered
to me.

I mean I could hear each stroke like a pointing finger

so that I could walk into the paint
or one side of me be there
like a nude faced frontally to show her bulges
flatly.

I pay attention to my fingernails
and   when the moons disappear and under the long
        part
yellow gets stuck
then I know it's time to be lonely.

You will think I am intentionally careless
and spontaneous.
You will love me,
describing the familiar bow-wow
as I make my plans.

Patricia Henley

KLAMATH FALLS, OREGON

To Grave, to Cradle

A small rain falls on lovers
lying in lambsquarter
caught in the bite
of the mother's moon tooth.
Tribal fire, tribal cries, burn nearby.
He is thunderbolt,
she, another source of light.
They come home, *come home*
to grave, to cradle
under ribs of rotting timber
creaking in wind.
Even in blaze burning palms & cheeks
as they touch, ash exists,
cold & inevitable.
In every beginning, an ending:
the salmon decaying on his bones
even as he spawns upriver,
the picked lilac in dust.

I walk to the post office
and see the mountain, a blue bone.
I want to show you the way
it resembles a fine lady's haircomb,

but we are apart, heart-sore
and inhabiting one another's dreams.
I have closed the door
on your daily politics,

the last minute search for the lost reader,
the noisy games. Over the phone
I say *I love you*. Soberly you answer, *no,
you don't*. We are each alone.

Stalemated, we hang up on the holiday.
A mother who loves but leaves,
I follow a path of question, a maze,
solitary route of empty phone booths.

Poem for Charley

eight years old

Thanksgiving we talk long distance.
You are excited in the season's first snow.
I imagine your chapped raw cheeks,
I hear the barking dog's staccato

and almost smell the cold
rolled in by your heavy winter clothes.
Here the air is sheer warm gold,
sweet with sunlight. Everyday

Poem for Suzanne

Among the Persian rugs & cushions,
the tea you offered,
the wine we drank,
what happened there?

You tell me what kind of woman you are.
I know this about you:
you are the woman who trails a white lilac
at her side, walking steps behind her man
in a dream he may never share.
The pollen of a lifetime floats around you,

veil of honey, *what may be*.
I am watching from my kitchen window.
The coffee thickens in the pot.

We could have been more polite
or distant
like stars in different galaxies.
Instead you lean so easily into my arms.

Let us brush one another's hair
until sparks fly!
Running home from you
after midnight
I see the bright rhododendrons glow
under moonlamp like exotic fish
set free
in a dark leafy sea.

Joanne de Longchamps

RENO, NEVADA

The Glassblower

The terrible black quarrels,
the flailing stick-words,
the familiar breaking of this marriage—
splintered glass.

Someone is entering the room,
coming with the sound of wind-chimes
or of a ruby ring
that clearly strikes on crystal.
It is love, the artisan, the glassblower
skilled with fire and breath
who takes our fragments into flame
and from the flame gives form.

Here is a little frigate in full sail.
Here are delicate brittle beasts and flowers
and now a new orb shines, a vessel
holding light once more.

Chocolate Waters

DENVER, COLORADO

I Feel So Good I Ain't Written a Fuckin' Thing in a Year

I feel so good I ain't written a fuckin' thing in a year.
The world isn't any more perfect.
Men are still beating their wives and dropping babies out of windows.
Nixon is running around doing a world tour—
    promoting his new book (and being cheered on by his mother).
Computers will soon be able to put the entire human race on microfilm.
We've got Wonder Woman now, and the Bionic Woman, even the Oil of Olay Woman,
And the multinationals are rapidly devouring what's left of the earth.
BUT

My lover hasn't left me.
So how do you write a poem about how your lover *hasn't* left you?
My lover Ronnie, wants me to write poetry, but I'm with *her*—
    who wants to write poetry?
My ex-lover is as creepy as ever, but I'm *sick* of writing poems about her.
My best friend, Linda, wants me to write something about how wonderful *she* is,
    but why should I do that? when all you have to do to find that out
    is ask her.
Reed says, "Write a poem about Allyson and Scruff-o."
    Do you care about Allyson and Scruff-o?
I care about Allyson and Scruff-o, but what am I going to write?
    . . . Scruff-o's nose was dry today
    and he runs around the apartment in his Morris T-shirt
    eating Red Seal potato chips.
    . . . Allyson is not allowed to bark like a real dog
    so she makes funny clacking noises with her teeth.

In July, I went to this hot-shit "poets' convention" in Port Townsend.
Emily Dickinson to the left of me Gertrude Stein to the right of me—
Mountains of perfectly composed 8½ by 11 typewritten sheets of paper
    about the amazing events of their unprecedented lives
    came pouring forth from their doors and windows at all hours of the day and night.

I, on the other hand, took many long walks by the straits of the Juan de Fuca,
    watched the sailboats come and go and talked voluminously to the seagulls,
AND
I felt so good
I may not write anything
for another fuckin' year.

Father Poem II

I wanted to *talk* to my father and he said,
"Look at that big fat nigger woman with the big fat titties."
(He was speaking of Aretha Franklin.)
I wanted to *talk to my father* and he said,
"You know that guy really did have noble intentions."
(He was speaking of Adolf Hitler.)
I wanted to talk to my father and he said,
"Why don't you get off your big ass, Lard Butt, and fix my dinner?"
(He was speaking to my mother.)
I wanted to talk to my father and he said,
"Two dykes used to own my bar, but we don't talk about queers in *this* family."
(He was speaking to me.)
I wanted to talk to my father and he said,
"We live in a sick society."
"*You* certainly do," I said,
(And I was speaking to myself.)

Adrianne Marcus

SAN RAFAEL, CALIFORNIA

The Child of Earthquake Country

My friend in the east says it's raining
back there. Temperature, mid-nineties,
thunderstorms at sea. He wears light tan
in this weather. Grey is for winter.
I tell him it's summer out here. The
early morning fog has burned off; the
sky is perpetual, blue. Don't you find
that weather boring, he asks? No.
Perfection is never boring, I tell him.
He says he could never make it out here.

He's right. He likes minor changes.
In weather. And I am a child of the
earthquake country, live on the edge
of San Andreas fault. Twice
I have woken up at night
feeling the house sway beneath me,
felt the earth shift,
rocking the foundations. Just
out of sleep, groggy, I realize
there is no time to fasten anything
into place. When it stops
rolling, I fall back asleep.

Even today, I look out my window
at the mountain. I can't swear for
certain it will be there tomorrow.
Earthquakes are unpredictable; all
I can be sure of is one thing:
it will happen again.

So I live in this positive, uncertain
house, on the unstable land. I say
when the house is firm: it is time.

Time to play. At being alive, at being
whatever I can be. While knowing
the land beneath me is building up
pressure, the tectonic plates
are going to slip, and when that
happens, look for a doorway to
get under. Wait it out. Nothing
is safe. And this is the way
I live. Where even the land redefines
itself, shock after shock. Where
civilization begins.

Grey: The Madness

"Madness is only Open Day in the factory of the
    mind. We
can walk through, prodding and touching, question-
    ing,
feeling wonder at the innumerable patterns of
    strangeness
which woven and processed, parceled and delivered,
    bear no
resemblance to the original materials, yet contain
    them and
are part of them."
    Janet Frame, *Scented Gardens for the Blind*

There is no welcome sign. No number
posted as to exact inhabitants
promised or residing in this place.
No dates. When it was founded
or by whom.

By whatever means you got here, car

or train, walking years until you thought
the destination lost, you do arrive.
And when you cross, another leaves,
taking your car or train to go further
into the interior. Without you.

At first you make mistakes. From
a distance you see what looks
like you. Closer, it turns out to
be a statue. Who carved it, you
wonder, then you notice a chisel
in your hand, particles of dust
embedded in your clothing.

You begin to work again. First,
the eyes, grey stone. You can't decide
what shape to make the mouth: a smile?
Tight lips? You can't take chances,
leave the mouth inside the stone.
It's easier to live in silence.
You drop the chisel, then the hammer.
They fall silently away inside the dust.

With luck you will forget.
The light will fall from grey
to grey again. You fall asleep
at last, refusing to hear voices
dream your name, until you have
forgotten how you came. Become
the silence. Leave for the interior.

"To Count a Million Objects, Even in 12 Years, One Cannot Spend Much Time on Each One."

The Clustering of Galaxies
Scientific American, November 1977

A dull grey man arrives, hands you his
card marked *Important*. He's come to cart
off year after year you've been saving.
He begins by putting the intricate minutes
into piles, then lifts the heavy coins which
have been struck into the shapes of clocks.
He stacks everything into sacks, calibrated

to hold just so much, a million incidents.
No more. No less.

He works without wasted motion. He is Swiss.
Disorder offends his senses. When he leaves
you he goes on to his other jobs, blessing
train schedules, assembly lines, the revised
trajectories of cause and effect.

If he spoke in a human voice all the
responsible numbers would fall into complete
patterns. But he says nothing. Mystery
is part of his act. It is enough to be
God of anything. Even counting.

It's Buffalo, Boise, or Boston This Time

Love, making love all night,
I think, this can't be Buffalo.
Morning comes and calls it Buffalo.
So much for fantasy. Get up. It's
time to leave.

At the airport, I assure you everything's
all right. I board the plane, alone.
So much for friendly skies. My life
is going forward. Why am I locked
in place, or else, reverse?

I need a sensible direction. This
waiting to arrive, this wondering
which airport has our names
and which motel, won't work.
We're beginning to resemble passengers,
anonymous as seats, with faces
only flight crews know by heart.

Instead of Buffalo, or Boise, Boston,
Philadelphia, why don't we meet,
not for an hour, or a one-night
stand, but something else?
Say, a place that has our names
and where the ink can dry.
I'll bring my pen. You bring
your signature along. We'll
sign both ways.

Letter from an Exile

This trip was unplanned. Nothing like Europe
this fall, or even the Greater Antilles.
Disassemble the fishing rod, unknot the
nylon that holds the bright hooks in place.
Lay them out; put them away. I could have
been fishing: I heard the thin snap, like
the line reeling out, whipping the air
before it hits water. Then I knew what
I'd caught: not a fish, but my foot.

Then the whole thing went crazy: the
invisible fish on the end of the line
when you're not looking, the entire
foot lifted in the air, dropped back
down, throbbing. I tell you, it was
more alive than I wanted, dangling
at the end of my leg.

What's left to do after all that? Put
things back into place. The receptionist
asks, "What happened to you?" as she watches
me limp into Emergency Room at four in the
morning. I was collecting things, I say,
I collected broken toes this week. Here's
one of my finest. Or Monopoly: when you
throw the dice thinking this time it's
two hundred dollars for passing Go. Instead,
you hit the wrong space, the wrong board
which directs you to the treatment room
and you end up in jail, the treatment room,
where the good doctor arrives, right after
the X-Ray and gives you the next roll of the
dice: Stay off that foot, don't move anywhere
else that might hurt. But I'm going fishing,
I tell him. He says, Really? Then you are
off, to this exotic vacation paradise, this
new port of call which is named House.
Then there's Bed. And there's Rest.
Three weeks or more to cruise back and
forth, and to write: Only my foot's gone on
vacation. Having a terrible time.
Wish I weren't here.

Kathleene West

PORT TOWNSEND, WASHINGTON

Striking Out

*"Then said Evangelist, pointing with his finger over
a very wide Field, Do you see yonder Wicket-gate?
The Man said, No. Then said the other, Do you see
yonder shining light? He said, I think I do."*
— *Pilgrim's Progress*

Believe the light, believe the eye,
the ant that detours a human foot.
She turns her face west, moves
as the sun would move
through slash and tight bushes
to the muddy clearing. Always a house,
unabandoned, a family of faces
knitted tight at the window.
Beyond, the watersick land falls down
to a brilliant sea.

Believe the curve of the earth,
those that swayed in ships and wagons
toward the end of water, the end of land.
The journey pulls not to an edge
or an inviting door
but here, on this open flat, where it began.
Still waving good-by,
the families group,
the backs of their hands clicking in time.
She tries to match the rhythm
but her hand thrusts out,
sure as a divining rod
and the people part for her like the sea.

Believe wind, the air that kisses

then rips the skin.
A hawk dips behind the one man she remembers,
wings frame his head,
disappear at his throat.
Air sucks back
and the large sky swallows a talon,
a mask. Her wrist aches
from the weight she once carried
and a sudden gust pushes her to the ground.

Believe water in thin lines of rain,
the sheen on a leaf,
sweat.
At the river she lays nothing down
and drinks from one cupped hand.
The river is a crease in her palm.
She traces it upstream,
chooses one small stream,
one source.

A choked sound escapes from the grasses
and waves shatter the shoreline.
In a tattered house, walls splinter
to etch out a map of the next country.
The road lights deep and straight
but she will clear her own path,
curving as the narrow stream curves.
On the river, people float down
on rented barges.
They are sleek and singing.
She believes their voices,
but lifts a fallen limb like another gate
and closes the path behind her.

Sheila Nickerson

JUNEAU, ALASKA

In the Alley: June

Yellow lilies,
White malamute straining
Against its rope:
Berries, hooded in green,
Hang like parachutes
Caught in a long green war.

Phyllis Koestenbaum

SAN JOSE, CALIFORNIA

Minor Poem

Going to Menlo Park
early, with time to spare,
I observe a dry sun.
I write it down:
dry sun.
dry.
giving nothing out.
contained. sun
more moon than sun.
alone up there.
I stop for buttons,
I need two.
then the freeway
where five miles beyond Menlo
Father Junipero Serra will look at you
as you look at him.
today I would find him rested
and routinely grave,
staring
from his distance;
but I am stopping at Menlo Park.
off the freeway a country stand
offers strawberries, stringbeans, lettuce.
not country,
and the road forces cars
to turn
like sleepless invalids.

Father, do you pray
for them, cars
and invalids.
I park on a side street to sew
buttons on my plain beige sweater:
old and droopy.
Entremont is playing and conducting
Mozart.
greedy Philippe.
I cut thread on the crack
of the almost empty spool,
leave thread
dangling.
no scissors.
the day is uncut too.
I walk to the building
where I am going
as if I am not
going there.
imagine where.
it has been painted barely brown.
it doesn't even smell new,
paint ground in wheels
of air.
a pity, I think,
the painter was gifted
like me
with a minor imagination.

Friday

I will answer he will say mother died my brother his voice will
tear he will say her head hurt she was afraid I am cold I expect
him to hurt me I am

expecting a telegram his voice tears he chews his fingernails
those habits cannot be broken wisteria wallpaper a maple dresser

old hair and thumb tacks discarded address books there are phones
in the bedrooms the phone rings in the kitchen

he tells me to make the orange juice first wash the container in
the sink soap strung around the water like a noose when I answer
Frances says you worry too much plastic melts in the dishwasher
Frances says I worry where is

Frances in dreams a friend Bruno Bettelheim will you defend me
Madeleine comes on Friday on Friday

I go to Dr. Fry Madeleine's breasts heave cold white uniforms to
clean in she leaves her coat open so we can see them I am missing
something dreams are tricky I sit down sometimes to peel potatoes
they fucked in the sauna Madeleine found them pig

she called whore she sleeps between the walls of my kitchen
in dreams there are no words but you hear them I am cold I answer
where is he when I need him she has no children she has no
mother she is forty I have tried to cover

the walls lemon and narcissus an orange and green abstract in a
yellow frame an asparagus fern to tickle them on their way to the
refrigerator the children are strong they don't like to be on their
way to market village women dangle string shopping bags mother

a light over the counter to sew by my kitchen pale as a child
with disease I answer the phone I have not been in a concentration
camp but I could have been I heard the words Bruno Bettelheim
on the telephone

Mary Crow

FORT COLLINS, COLORADO

Montserrate

They climb the mountains on their knees
Dirty, their patched pants
breaking open
the dark faced lady sobbing
A child holding his crutch over his head
hauls his body up a foot at a time
and the sky is so beautiful
full of green fingers of pine
the clean clouds
and a color like the blue of church windows
On top, in the church,
racks of tiny candles,
50 pesos each,
burn for the dead
for the living
and in the dark church
the moreno Christ is darker
blood streams down his arm
down his leg
and the people think he is theirs
Plastic protects Christ's knees
from their dirty caresses

They have crawled up here,
their bloody knees burn
and they too have drops of sweat
on their foreheads and backs
Here they are in this skyey church
in their temple of trees
the slough of wind a kind of music
and the white and blue of sky, church, and Mary,
is a cleanness they desire
But the Christ, Christ of Sorrows,
collapsed above the pulpit

leans on his arm
and can hardly raise his head
to look at them
They have left their crutches
their walking sticks
here for him, here for love,
and think they will walk again
without that cross
Urchins pass through the pilgrims
just coming up,
looking for tourists
or tear-careless worshippers
their faces hard
and their eyes beady as Christ's

The Heat in Medellin

In the parque Beiria
the armless and legless
are laid out by the church,
their sad eyes
look up from grey pallets.
Dirty children are waking
from their concrete beds
over the warm air vents
and the blind man
calls out his lottery numbers.
Morning in Medellin
and my heart is already hard.
Rubber stamps drum in the bank
and the eyes of waiting people are dull.
As I leave, a woman walks up,
stark naked, and people laugh
and say she is crazy.

She walks into the reflecting pool,
her dimpled flesh quivering, oblivious,
and I envy her.
In Junin the kiosks display
pale freesias with their smell of death;
stiff yellow callas for the grave
are being watered
while the suburbs have no water,
and the poor drink
from the stinking river.
Every morning we read
about the children who died.
And there is no light either
because the rains are late this year.
Glass stands sell peaches and grapes
imported from Chile,
imported from California.
Further down the block the vendor
makes the sign of the cross
over his cigarettes
as he begins his day.
Morning in Medellin,
and a man in rags sits down on the sidewalk
and lifts his trousers
so we can pity his open wound.
Morning in Medellin,
and here comes the crazy man in his rags,
bearing his cardboard box
with the red chicken and the white,
one pink rose, a small flag, and a ribbon
arranged on top. He holds it up
as he talks to God
from his perfect world.

My Barrow Stones

I live on an island
and there I tend
a little heap of stones.
I keep busy
rearranging them.
Sometimes
I pile them up
to form
a rocky phallus
pointing skyward,

a cairn
marking the way
to nowhere.

Or I arrange them
in rings
signs of eternity
or concord
circles
circling each other
embracing earth
enclosing nothing.

I have wrung them
and gotten
sore hands:
They would not cry.
I have rubbed them
but they would not
catch fire;
hacked them
but they would not
shape up.

Sometimes
I plant my stones
in the rocky soil,
make a sign
at the sun
to make
my stones grow.

I dig them up.
After all,
I have
to live
on this island.

Not Volcanoes, Not Minerals

I am being followed.
Actually, I'm hardly aware
of the faint footsteps behind me.
Laughing too loud,
I don't hear

the scurrying of animals.
I can't see the light in the car
parked beside the forest
as I lie down in the dark.
Bundles of twigs for my bed,
I look up at the horned moon.
A moth with fabulous markings,
gold and black,

I rise out of the darkness
on the path of the moon.
Fish flutter in the deep water
behind my eyelids
waking me out of myself,
and I see a man
watching me, writing down
what I am.

Adrien Stoutenburg

SANTA BARBARA, CALIFORNIA

Icarus on Wheels

I have been measuring miles all day
(on maps, in my mind)
their ruts and detours,
their crawl toward summits
where timber loses its breath;
their rush down slopes
to where cross-winds whirl
hitchhikers and birds off balance;
and the way roads run
both toward and from
the place I have marked
(on the map, in my mind)
before cold sense—
acid as sorrow—
makes all routes reel back
on their asphalt spools.

Yet, in my dream of flight
I keep driving on,
a maniac of time
counting gas stops, motels,
signs that predict the way,
until the fan of distance closes
just where the sun burns down
upon one passionate, waiting face.

I shed the world. I soar
through light-years, night-years,
self-blinded, a growing torch . . .

But in my second dream . . .
to freeze, to fall,
to smell the lugging earth

and bitter ice,
to crash,
a clutch of ashes in my hand.

The car waits in its husk,
a metal beast, its tires worn bare.
I struggle toward it
and the miles going back:
invisible but there
                    but there.

Riding Hood, Updated

There had to have been a wolf that night,
alive in his rank fur and throat,
ears twigged, wild feet leaving flowers
on spring-deep earth. The howl was there;
his shadow kept house behind every bush.

Remember, dead grandmother,
me in my hood, and the old rifle swinging
between us, ready for that hot tongue's flash?
There was a moon, too, skull-shaped but red.
Clouds leaned against it,
and the pines were windy harps.
A lake beckoned blue somewhere
like sky at the end of a downhill road.

There must have been an owl as well,
feather-corseted, hinged with claws;
and a bobcat's cry.

Who knows what other things lurked there?

It is nothing now to you,
snug in your bonnet of earth,
out of the howl, forever wolf-free.
Here where the hunt goes on,
and unimaginable beasts are loose,
it's different for me.

River Boat

It surprised the night and me
like a suburb of lights
gone suddenly adrift.
Its searching beam,
a long, white spy sent out ahead,
probed trees, backwashes, drunken logs,
set weeds on fire,
and dazzled even mud to sparks.

Ignorant of broader craft
than common rowboat or canoe,
I blinked like a desert toad,
and held my breath
as it drummed near,
its deliberate bulk
strung with electric fireflies
to warn the darkness from its path.

"An ordinary Mississippi barge,"
my river-wise companion said.

No. What glided there
was a fallen freight of stars
that put the wind ablaze
and burned—and stays.

Memory Album

When this you see,
Remember me.

Memory is a miser, spendthrift, thief,
unearthing entire sepulchers,
blind cottonwoods, murmur of kitchen stoves,
geranium smell of musty living rooms,
the millinery sign that creaked
outside the shopworn house
where I read fairytales
while rain invented curtains on the wind.

Procession of farmers, merchants,
fishermen: a tramp with sooty eyes
at a back door, and wives with scattered hair
and soap-red hands;
old Bill, the ram, who butted when provoked,
tin cowbells beating in the pines,
the gasping freight below the water tank,
the depot where a metronome
clicked out its constant messages
of birthdays, marriages, and death.

I know each name. This one died on a train
(the scalpel showed a rusted heart);
another, lovetorn, blew his brains apart
rather than face a simpering girl's disdain;
and those with tumors, those with bitten nails;
widow, hustler, saint, the simple, and the sly,
fathers, cousins, friends, all with one cry:
"Remember me! Remember me!" The past exhales

their mingled breath, and even the hot scent
of sunflowers wearing halos meant
for loftier deities. All images are bent
through time, and some most prized are fraudulent—

as mine may be. Remember this, if you remember me.

Colleen McElroy

SEATTLE, WASHINGTON

Flight

The land is flat
And my head throbs.
Inside, I am motionless
As I flee
The farms and thoroughbred
Houses.
Crossing another town
And crossing still another.

Inside, I am still
And the quiet throbs
Between my clenched teeth.
My arms ache,
Long to be wings.

I take my annual flight
Like some extinct black bird
Looking for a nesting place.
You are home
And your token kiss,
Your icy eyes are left behind

Along with that coldly blessed
Check—payment for my blackness.
I also left my token smile
Tossed behind the kitchen door.
I am running

And remember the child
Who waved goodbye on the stairs.
Her eyes button black,
Her legs long as mine.
Inside, I am quiet

Staring out
Curiously as the cat

Whose green eyes insist
On following me
As I pass these towns.

Morning in Argentina

(for Helen)

poems in hand, I follow
Helen's camera
from the carbon soaked hillsides
of Zipaquira
to the Plaza San Martin
where cobblestones are ancient
as death

we no longer trust what we see—
tourist hotels
are as legal as government houses,
their palisades so full
of civilized glory
we almost fail to see
the famous poet tracing hedgerows
of trailing vines with his white cane

the camera records the scene
and for one second
Borges is frozen in a cloak of bright
Sunday colors—
pigeons walk with a child's innocence,
their up and tuck steps
reflected in murky ripples of shallow puddles,
their chalky eyes blindly tilted
toward the West

only the poor
choke in this land of good air,

69

this place of big waters
and Spanish conquerors
that no longer reflects its Indian fathers—
picture postcards are filled
with boleros and tanned leathers
while the stark white domes of cathedrals
bleed into the shadows
of battle ready guns

Borges what do you see with your inner eye—
a personal anthology of Indian names
in a town where all the Indians have vanished,
a riot of imaginary beings romping
in the lush green of Amazon fables,
anything but the actual scene—
the prophecy of lands where fallen leaves
stare at us with dead eyes—
we are all blind
and the birds will not weave
our memories into morning

When Poets Dream

they come dressed in bones
in feathers
in stanzas of social concern
they roll syllables
between thin sheets
of rough paper
twisting and binding the bundles
with Houdini images
they wait for spring
then brood when it comes
on dreamless nights
they use slivers of a fogbound moon
to reduce mountains into snow cones
of powdered sugar
they are tender children
born of caesura
jealous and backbiting
as eels
like bacteria
they have no internal membranes
except for digestive vacuoles
those hollow sacs of words
that will suck you inside
poems that sing
and stories full of dark green rhythms
they are all mad

all of them   the poets
they do not know the world is flat
and full of fast food

Catacombs: Dream Poem Number One

Bradford Lindstrom was once Wall Street
and rich to the bone,
his herring grey mustache and Dow Jones
figure neatly trimmed to match
ledgers of money.
Now he is my neighbor and alcoholic,
his hands red and seedy with shaking.
Our bedrooms touch wall to wall,
rubbing each other's silences.
Some days I see him moving toward
the mailboxes,
his face reflecting the confusion
of all those rows of silver vessels
marking the forty odd residents
of this building
and banked like metal coffins;
the whole mess stacked high enough
to keep out any flooding waters,
like those tombs in Buenos Aires
or New Orleans.

He doesn't know which is his,
so I lend him my key
and we watch scraps of paper
flutter to the floor like lost birds—
retirement brochures addressed
to occupant,
scrawled postcards from old friends
who've almost forgotten his first name;
Dear B. L. they begin,
the redness spreads from hands
to neck and face as he hurriedly
gathers them up.
I turn away fumbling
with my own bulging mass
of rejections from distant critics.
Sometimes in the softness
of early morning dreams,
I hear him tap tap
on the walls
quickly gently
telling me he loves me still.

Joan LaBombard

LOS ANGELES, CALIFORNIA

August

We have hung this house with roses
And scattered the shimmering webs to catch his light.

For fox cubs leap in his footprints;
He walks where the lions wake
Lifting their blazing, flowery heads
In the secret wheat.

He walks with the ring-necked pheasant
And the spotted deer
In the perfect bell of the day like the only note,
The richest resonance;
He knows where the nests are hidden—
Where the ruby-throat and the emerald sing together.

We have spun soft down of the peacock's colors
To feather his bed,
His lion's lair—

We have heaped this house with roses, with foxes'
    fur
For the lord of light.

The Covenant

Some covenant is broken.
The one that speaks of leaves
like green hands bursting
from a child's drawing of stick trees
The one that promises
after clouds, light walking the fields
falling in pillars,
how sun
will unlock the trout
from their cold prison
The covenant that says
this train rumbles on, as it should,
toward known towns and the names we remember,
the depots brilliant with summer
and everyone there
smiling and waving—
That covenant
which never hinted at
this slow glide backward through a snowy landscape
past black barns, and the stations dark,
the sign over each depot banging
loose in the wind,
and none familiar,
while the lights of the strange towns
wink out one by one.

In the Old City: Dubrovnik

Suddenly in the square by Onofrio's Small Fountain
The pigeons rose in a gust of wings, lifting
Over our startled heads, to the rapt cries of children;
Wheeling in one long ripple of motion
Like a grey shawl shaken over us, and interwoven with light,
They circled the square three times
Storming the old facades in a blizzard of wings,
Brightening gaunt stone, clouding the air with feathery brilliance
So that our eyes smarted
And wingbeats pulsed in our ears,
Then, as suddenly, dropped in a grey, diminishing drift
Down at our feet, comically to resume
Their feeding and strutting.
Oh the soft birds, cries the child, scattering breadcrumbs.
But they printed a vision of strangeness on my mind:
The air full of wings
                              and rushing sound,
Like a myth I almost know,
Sunlight on worn stone,
And the fountain rising and falling at the heart of it.

Elaine Dallman

RENO, NEVADA

A Parallel Cut of Air

Your hand moves
a parallel cut of air,
touches the falling motion
from your hair.
You put the hair back in line
and fade again.

It is a trick of yours.
You handled each detail.

I think of you
over my stretch of walnut
desk. I think how you can
arrive here.

I have a mind full of people.
So many. Some move, some partly move.

It is a trick of mine
down the long years.

Later

High bare white walls
and the facts of separation.
We talk of our ex-spouses.
We believed marriage shook bells of incense.

We talk. My cousin told me of how you stared
down the aisle of vespers.
You clasped the rail. It would have bruised
if it had been a wrist.

I return your patched coverlet,
your dried-out auto-glove,
your blue beret from the Basque country.

You are the traveler, with tales of escape.
Your eyes are harder—
the way the film of incandescent porch light
mingles with city air.

Phyllis Thompson

HONOLULU, HAWAII

Rainwater

for Herbert Applebaum

The shades are pulled, but still I hear the rain. Under the streetlight
The street glistens in my mind, burnished in the same rainwater
That has been coming back

Since the first cloud-cover drenched the first burning stone of the world.
The same rain, its common shining. But this night is singular.
I want to hold it.

Yet it is not this night but you I want to keep, miracle
In the century of my own life, safe to the centuries
After, just as you are—

The very gesture of your hands pushing back through your white hair,
Or your teeth biting your under lip as you dance, your eyes held
On an inward vision.

I've imagined you Israeli, kin to those chosen of God
Who live where the rock of origin remembers oldest rains
And remembers also

Jerusalem's complicated history. And what is saved
Out of the vanished eras for them to know, just as it was?
Only the rainwater.

What's human within those faiths which live in our age from that source,
Once real as the beautiful names of Israel, is lost sight of,
Is general as the rain.

Even for my own need I can't find words to fasten down
An image strong enough to carry you clear of time, exact,
Recognized as yourself.

The historical, the human, leaves the powerful symbol,
Dies. But the rain comes back always the same. When you have left me,
I will imagine the rain, and it will be as I imagine.

Ann Stanford

BEVERLY HILLS, CALIFORNIA

The Fountain

You must remember never to offend the gods
by being too sure of anything.
Think of Niobe, how she grew in pride
watching her seven tall sons and seven fair daughters.

Who would not? Having created such
superb heads set on the pure columns
of the necks, the long hair glistening in the sun
and their voices musical as water

in a bright stream rippling over rocks—
the archer, the runner, the studious,
the orator, the weaver, the gatherer of garlands,
one with his horse, another at the lyre,

wherever she looked she saw the gold
limbs of her children, strong
in the sun, their laughter
beyond the sounds of the strings, even the chords

Orpheus struck before he lost his bride
before he disobeyed the charge of Hades
and looked back into the dark
where Arachne in a still corner wove

over and over the stories of the gods
and their offenses, how Hades caught
Persephone, and Leto's son
killed one by one the children of Niobe.

Composing the Garden

I

Start with the bounds. What's to go out or stay.
The view you'll keep, the lake, the fading ranges.
Columns of cypress shield the western slope,
as for the south, arrange a grove of olives.
On the north, white oleander
can form a wall beside the avenue.
Over the walk you put an arch of vines.
You must be firm with space. Even the sky
becomes your own.

Divide the sky, let it be lanes or views,
parterres, or rounds of blue above the pool.
Cut it with branches, winter-white, in shapes
of leaded glass, break it with scattered leaves
into shimmering drops, or panes
between the arches of the hedge, or dark with lines
or circles from your vista under the trees.
You've set the bounds, laid out the earth and sky.
Whatever you do, things will not stay this way.

II

You must get back to the plan
the central theme, the axis of the garden
that great effect each part must be subject to.
You can pull it together

by a great stairway perhaps,
breaking across the terraces, holding them like a knot
around a bundle.
Or a major prospect. You must frame the view
between windows of laurel
or a balustrade at the edge of the terrace;
don't let it simply slide away.

If the terrain allows, you may put a central walk,
say, down to the lake. The slope will give you streams
from the upper cascade, a suite of stairs and lawns and pools,
that rise in fountains—a dolphin or seahorse, a goddess
surrounded by naiads, or an arched tower
from which the flow thunders into whirlpools.
At angles to the axis will be corridors
between gardens of cypress, holm oak, chestnut, or cedar;
these passages lead into gardens
each with its focus—statue, flower bed, sundial.

Or let the main path be a corridor
between privet; the clipped alleyways
lead to quiet openings beside lilyponds.
Or a central fountain, or a stair uphill
to a portico over the blue paving of the lake
with its grand vista fronting the water,
the terrace leading to the belvedere,
formal and open, inviting by its long straight paths
the gaiety of sunlight, the mock of shadow,
the white admonition of the statues.

III

But it must make sense. The mad cascade
the storm dropped yesterday has ruined the parterres.
They're sunk in mud, the stairways slipping with dirt and leaves.
Everything drips—the eaves, the edges of trees, the hedges.
It was more than a water garden, a meeting of too many streams.
After a day of sun, you can clean out the paths
wash off the terraces, put drains where streams carried away the soil.
But today while the clouds decide whether to go or stay
get to details. What is the garden made of?
Planes, levels, paving, paths, trees and hedges,
low plantings and high, sun and shade, color and light.

Down by the lake already there are beeches and oaks,
a drift of wild cyclamen. Farther up for sun
plant a spread of lantana, a border of lilies;
on the end of the terrace, magnolias; by the reflecting pool
urns of geraniums, plumbago, purple

bougainvillaea, vases of lemon set on balustrades
and hedges of laurel, cypress, holly.
For the old walls, jasmine, clematis, honeysuckle, roses
beside iris and loquat, oleanders, mandarins.
For autumn color, liquidambers, persimmons, against the pine trees.
Pomegranate and flowering thyme,
lavender, shrub roses, fuchsias
and wisteria on the steeper banks.
You will want mimosa and orange trees
the acrid scent of alders by the stream.

But your list is already too long
and you've left no room for the kitchen garden.
You've forgotten the plan, the cool laying out of the ground.
You've overwhelmed the garden, unthinking as any god.

IV

Things can get so easily out of hand.
Whatever you do, you must keep order.
Here where the horses broke through things have gone to ruin.
Refugees camped here, the statues are lost
or broken. The lilies dragged from the pond
where they washed their rags and their children.
They burned the hedges for firewood
cooking thin gruel, warming their hands,
blackening the wall behind the fires.
It was frosty those nights. The temple of Demeter
hung with bedclothes to keep out the wind,
her columns slant with ropes,
the goddess fallen. Boots chipped her fingers,
her torch carried away, her basket broken.

Up by the terrace wall some spread their tents
with poles of cut cypress. They thatched them with branches.
Boys pushed the urns from the terrace
carved their names on the wall.
Sheep and goats nibbled the thyme of the parterre
ate the leaves of hydrangeas;
and cows tethered to the columns of the balustrades
pulled them out like ragged teeth.
The garden disappeared in mud and slime
and the trample of feet.
But the old ilexes remain
their twisted roots hold the rifts of a wall
built by the emperor. This was ruin before.

Now you begin.

V

Yes, it is getting harder.
The easy part was beginning,
dreaming the garden, but it is midday
and there's much to do
more perhaps than you are able.
The ground where you dig has become harder,
the tangle of laurel beyond keeps out sunlight.
You stand on the long terrace
where the ground was trampled
under so many feet.
When you began, it did not seem this way
the shovel went into the loam, into the soft
leavings of leaves.
        The lake is farther away
and the boat has disappeared.
The cloud coming up from the west
throws a shadow on the lake;
it goes dull like a piece of chiseled slate.
Rain will bring mud; you'd better dig
while there's still time. You look at the stains
where fire burned the wall,
the graffiti, and the torn balustrades.
What are you doing? How did you get here?
Your arms ache. You must bring leaves
and manure, gravel for paths.
You started so bravely. All you did was dream.
You dreamed the garden. Start now.
There is time.

Tomorrow you can put up the statues
mend the broken urns, take another look
at the long vista you first thought of.

VI

It is too cold to work.
No one cares anyway you tell yourself.
It's your garden, if it lies
forever undone, that's your business.
It's only for joy. You are tired
of the stubborn limbs all greedy for light
knotting themselves, choking one another.
The ground, baked hard, cracking in the sun,
and the creatures around and underground
waiting for something to grow.
Birds mock you from the trees, daring you like the others.

The lake has gone down to a stinking pool
edged with mud. The boat rots on the shore,
the seams break open in air, weeds hold the anchor chain
and the sky is neither sun nor cloud
but brown at the edges, pale at the center,
and a thick haze fills the gaps between the mountains.

If anyone cared, you repeat,
you might untangle the wood, close up the passageways
to the underground, rip out the vines
that strangle the trees, the thorny weeds, if anyone,
you say again, if anyone.

Going to Sleep

You stretch out
flat on your back
you say Ah!
this is not like anything else.

First, eye shuts a door
closes the window
reflects nothing
the headlights far off
come round a turn
go off again
a small thinning of dark.

Ear waits for a quiet house
admits the tap of rain
the rush of wind
owl cries.

Then you float off
toward a lake's dark center
find yourself struggling
drifting, rising up
holding hard to some torn-up
piece of yourself
you found there.

Crisis

Whatever this is, you have only this moment to do
    it in.
You must decide. The shadow of the hawk
rumples over the grass, splits on sharp stones;
the wave hangs motionless
spitting at the stiff edge, ready.

Only this between the descent
through the broken air, the water already
roaring and the knife-edge beak
breaking over the grassy shore.

Be brief. It is time to put out a hand
against the hawk, the wave.
Can you no longer hear
the shadow rattle the grass, the sea dividing?

Caught like a stone in the hawk's eye, the tunnel of
    water,
the ice wall of this unchangeable moment.

On Ann Stanford

BY JOAN JOHNSTONE

RECOGNITION CAME EARLY to Ann Stanford. When she was twenty, Yvor Winters, poet, programmatically rigorous critic, and her teacher at Stanford University, presented ten of her poems among the carefully, almost harshly sifted contents of *Twelve Poets of the Pacific* (New Directions, 1937). Winters introduced this collection of verses composed on clearly defined themes and in rhymed stanzas and regular meters, stating with equal force and generosity the poetic of the little group for whose best work he forecast permanency with distinction: "in the matter of conception, clarity, as opposed to contemporary obscurantistic tendencies . . . ; in the matter of style, purity and freedom from mannerism, as distinct from the contemporary tendency to substitute mannerism for true originality." The qualities he describes—clarity, purity, and ease—remain with Ann Stanford's poetry; the rhymes, predictable meters, and expository themes do not.

Reading these early works, one admires the young poet who so fully achieved a rational form of the brief lyric and whose intelligence gave value to the form. The common motive in these poems is reflective thought consequent upon accurate description and colored by appropriate, usually sober, feeling. The thoughts tend to reflect unavoidable, and thus familiar truths (for example, that the limits of perception waste experience, "On Sleep"), while the descriptions are sharp and distinctive, pulling truth out of the world itself, as when a hummingbird composes itself to sit for a moment, "Insolent, devoid of tune." (The Hummingbird)

Accurately, thoughtfully, Ann Stanford's poems fill out a landscape of California. It is an environing landscape in which details have meaning and consequences, where a mid-winter roadside can shine like a divine manifestation (Weeds, *The Descent*):

Nothing so startles us as tumbleweeds in December
Rising like ghosts before us in the headlamps
The big round weeds blowing into fences
Into guard rails and wheels, wedged into corners
Drifting in ranks over roads in a gusty order
Round in the orbits of winter, dropping the invisible seed,

Blown green and purple-leaved into springtime, soft with water,

Filled to harsh circles in the thirsty summer
Dried brown and jagged, ready for December
When the silver globes, magnificent in procession
Slow and solemn-paced in the ritual of ending
Dry, dead, in the dim-most part of the year
Spread the great round promises of green morning.

Always intense, the interaction between humans and nature is not always full of promise. In "Listening to Color" (*In Mediterranean Air*) even autumn's blue renewal takes place in a mildly sinister landscape of "sick/sky" and "white / sweet poison flowers." More typical are poems that record the shock of a world just lost, a fresh, expansive, irrecoverable countryside as near and far as a walnut grove (The Walnuts, *The Weathercock*) remembered from childhood by the poet, who returns

. . . an exile, knowing every turn
And turning home, and lost in the dazzled road
The strange, swept premises, and the great trees gone.

Grounded in place, the social bearings of Ann Stanford's poems are past-looking and deeply aware of social cohesion. Often the note of elegy recurs: for family members and family places; for President Kennedy and the navigator Magellan; for the destruction of culture, as in the sack of Troy (The Burning of Ilium, *In Mediterranean Air*)—

> . . . the bells scattered,
> the roofbeams fallen, lost, separate,
> moving somewhere under the wine-dark sun

—or for the wreck of the great libraries of Thebes and Monte Cassino. Horses move from a suburban paddock to fields still in the country; other horses are lost to sight, a "flying herd," drawn by a child on a wall, painted over, "sealed in stillness," "secret as the packet sealed with chain / To the courier's wrist." (Hidden Things, *The Weathercock*)

These elegies are intensely active poems. Proust-like, the poet lives only a transparency apart from the past. Also, classically, the dead have restless spirits. They make claims (To Her Spirit at the Winter Solstice, *The Descent*):

> . . . you force me in the cold to gather red berries
> Up early in mist, breaking the branches—
> The musky smell of the toyon—
> Will this be enough?

Spirit itself makes claims; it is astonishingly, anachronistically, convincingly present, as in the retelling of a mystical vision of Benvenuto Cellini, imprisoned below ground and longing for sun (The Artist Underground, *In Mediterranean Air* or in Night of Souls, *The Descent*):

> I saw each soul as light, each single body
> With his life's breath kindled and set like flame
> Before his nostrils. All creatures visible—
> Small beings moving in the midnight grasses,
>
> Light in the thoroughfares underfoot
> The mole's house hung with the mole's breath
> As with candles, and the busy air
> Clouded with light.

A translation? A recreation of perished sentiment, as if for a Williamsburg of the mind? Yet the diction is so simple and precise that one takes the vision for reality.

While feminist politics are engaged in a struggle against history, one may ask how such a conservative poetry suits the times. Unquestionably, Stanford's conservatism has focused on feminist concerns of long tenure. For example, in the late fifties she began working on an anthology of women poets in English. At the time "there had not been an anthology based on the inclusion of women important historically or by virtue of their intrinsic merit during this century." (acknowledgments, *The Women Poets in English*) Her polished collection of more than 130 poets offers notes on the poets' lives and a succinct, densely informative historical introduction. It brings to attention neglected poets like Mary Sidney Herbert (Countess of Pembroke), Charlotte Mew, and Emma Lazarus; unacknowledged ones like ballad singer Anna Gordon Brown of Falkland; and poets half-forgotten or scarcely known, like Fanny Kemble, Helen Selina Sheridan, and Helen Sorrells. It is a work of social value, reminding one that conservatism can be both independent and dynamic.

Then, too, some of her own poems take account of the very serious, even terrible, consequences of biological gender. In a substantial series of monologues, "The Women of Perseus" (*In Mediterranean Air*), the women of the myths speak of their fatal assignment: Andromeda, the virgin offered to a monster ("It is grim being a sacrifice,"); Medusa, raped by a god and transformed forever by her anger and disgust into the stony-eyed, snake-haired horror; Danae, a threatening daughter, a forgotten lover, and a desperate mother, nailed in a box to die at sea:

> Starve, drown, suffocate.
> These are my gifts
> from my father who starved me of love
> from my lover who drowned me in love
> from my son for whose birth I die in this stinking box.

Yet Stanford's tendency is to observe the contradiction, to balance extremes, and to search for those universal truths that reconcile opposites. So Perseus, too, has a speaking role, to tell of his accidental birth and circumstantial burdens. So, too, another monologue of terror, "The Beating" (*The Descent*), establishes a speaking voice without gender or place, a mind reduced to its held secret and its struggle against pain.

The variety of Stanford's personae illustrates again

the dynamic character of her conservatism: tradition serves her and not the other way round. A poet of the reasoned lyric composed in a plain style, that is, of a tradition reaching to the sixteenth century, she draws out the strengths of the tradition to make them serve her own style. Like Gascoigne and Anne Bradstreet, she writes with directness, economy, and restraint. Like them she is exact and subtle in diction, yet easy, unselfconscious, serious, and dramatic by turns, as if in conversation with her reader. At the same time, she has developed her own verse line, accommodating the close, rhymed forms of the earlier lyricists to freer modern forms.

During the late sixties, as she was making a verse translation of the *Bhagavad Gita*, Ann Stanford was coming to manage the line that dominates in her poems. It is a flexible, unrhymed syllabic line (she describes it in her introduction to the translation), yet it is also an elegant and formal line, in part because, like the earlier poets of the plain style, Stanford usually keeps the syntactical units of her line whole.

Ann Stanford has extended the range of her personae's conversations with the reader as she has mastered her line. Many of her poems of the sixties and seventies are linked in series, like "Composing the Garden" (included here). Sometimes the series are almost closet drama. Sometimes the persona is a single voice, as in sonnets or meditations. This latter voice, a brilliant invention, can be hieratic like the personae of Yeats, or a *voyeur* (as in the spy poems of *In Mediterranean Air*), or a witness. In "An American

Gallery" (*The Descent*) the speaker, chorus-like, re-creates a series of paintings and engravings, observing and commenting on the scene, setting it in time, and implying its meaning or coming fate.

These poems draw life from history, an achievement close to Ann Stanford's imagination. In "The Lecture" (*The Descent*), a witty poem of academic life, she praises Professor Leon Howard as, "Relaxed at the podium," he conjures an invisible America out of the darkness:

> "Strike through the mask," he cried, just short of the hour.
> And the stone heart warmed in two hundred breasts
> And the dark blood seeped up from under Hawthorne's leaves.

Reasoned, controlled, Ann Stanford's poetry expresses with subtle articulation historical and moral perceptions grounded in a sense of place and a sense of person. In a California that includes "marvelous Marin" and other approximations of the Land of Cockaigne, her arduous clarity rings like a tuning fork.

JOAN JOHNSTONE is a Lecturer in English at Stanford University. She has taught at many universities and colleges, including the University of California at Berkeley where she received her Ph.D. With William Chace she is the compiler of *Making It New*, an anthology of twentieth-century American poetry (Canfield Press).

An Interview with Ann Stanford

BY BARBARA GLENN

Question: You've moved with a great deal of ease—at least, apparent ease!—between scholarship (a study of Anne Bradstreet, an anthology of women poets, articles and reviews) and poetry, and then, in the poetry, from the stuff of the Greek myths to details of contemporary domesticity and solitude, from a translation of *Bhagavad Gita* and a verse play, *Magellan*, to the colloquial speech of some of your most recent poems. Can you talk about how you've moved from subject matter to subject matter, about the relationship of the various crafts of the scholar, poet, translator, and imaginative historian?

AS: I like scholarship, and translating—it's restful, like doing crossword puzzles—and I like feeling my way into the past, how it was to be a person then. So when I'm doing one thing, I'm often tempted to move to another kind of activity, to move along several paths, rather than just one. And then, there's coincidence, an idea coming as a result of a chance meeting with someone or of reading something that suggests a poem or essay or translation. I began *Magellan* because I read an account of his life in a magazine and became fascinated with his determination to reach a highly imaginative and difficult goal. I wanted to translate his journey into something resembling a spiritual quest.

Question: Besides *Magellan* and Anne Bradstreet, are there other historical figures or heroines that you've written about or would like to write about? I remember your poem about Anne Hutchinson which appeared in *The Southern Review*.

AS: I wrote another poem right after *Magellan*—of equal length, perhaps longer, certainly more complex, about a woman undergoing all kinds of trials to keep her principality for her son. It's called "The Countess of Forli." It goes right along with *Magellan*; the themes are similar. I was reading about the Medicis and I was intrigued by her story. I've written many poems with women in them: Niobe, Medusa and Danae—and then, real mothers and daughters.

Question: Do you consciously change speech patterns with your different subjects?

AS: I don't think of changing patterns of speech when I change subject matters. I like to think—"now, how is this person going to react if this person's a real person—sort of a person in two times—my time and her or his own time"—and I just let it come. It's hard, really, to talk about it—how you do things—because you really don't know. If you sit down and figure out how you do it, you miss.

I have, however, experimented with verse forms in the "An American Gallery" series, trying to get a rough line and texture. Sometimes I think that series is overlooked when people find my poetry so calm. Maybe it's because the violence there is resolved.

Question: What were the sources of those poems?

AS: The world is a violent place, and really a very frightening place if you think about it, and so you have to try to put that into human terms. *The Descent* is a book with a lot of violence in it. I wrote it during a decade in which there was a lot of protest. In this decade the atmosphere is different; my poems are different—I'm going into gardens.

Question: A retreat?

AS: No. It's just that I like gardens and it's about time I wrote about them.

85

Question: I don't want to pursue exclusively literary influences on your poetry. You've written about gardens for many years, and they seem rooted—no pun intended—very much in your heritage as a southern Californian.

AS: Yes. I would be pleased if you found a particular geographic place in my poems because I try to be specific and feel that I don't always succeed.

I've always been interested in gardens. My mother was a great gardener. I think a lot of women are influenced by their mothers. My mother I consider a very great woman. She was an Irish skeptic, a very good woman.

I've always felt that California's very much like Greece, even though I've never been there, and like the rest of the Mediterranean. California's like Portugal, too. I was there only once and it reminded me of home. The most important places to me are the places where I live. The people I live with— my friends and family—are all associated with place, too. The landscape, southern California— it's central in a way to my poems. I need the feeling, I think, of a kind of rural recognition, the surroundings of trees and plants, things happening outdoors. Even when I'm indoors.

Question: Another garden—you told me you were working right now on Anne Bradstreet's garden, trying to reconstruct it from what we know or can find out now.

AS: Oh, yes. Working on Anne Bradstreet's garden, if she had one, is a mystery, a puzzle. I like mysteries. I like detective stories because of the puzzle. I like to figure out who did it. That's the kind of scholarship I really like, where you try to find out something that's happened, rather than criticism.

Some of the poems of *In Mediterranean Air* are an outgrowth of my reading detective stories and spy stories, too. The spy just came to me. One day I wrote a poem about the spy, or about this couple watched by the spy. Next I wrote another poem about one of them watched by the spy. Then I thought I'd better write from the point of view of the spy. When I got to him out there in the garden, he became the one that I was most interested in. He just appeared, and I was very happy for a few days going down every morning writing a spy poem and putting him in different situations.

Question: You and others have remarked it is at last "time" for the recognition of women's achievements in poetry. I want to return for a moment to your anthology, *The Women Poets in English*.

AS: I got the idea for the anthology around 1957. I wanted to show that there are and were good women poets writing and they have been ignored. I wanted to get women into the mainstream.

While working on the anthology, I was interested to discover that there weren't any special things that women were writing about, or were unable to write about. The only thing excluded—and I mentioned it in the introduction—was war, which most women hadn't experienced, or up to that time hadn't experienced in the same way men had. And women's love poetry at that time, before all the liberation of today, was not as outspoken as it is now.

Question: In several places in your books, you've acknowledged opportunities to spend time at Yaddo, the writers' colony. For women especially, the idea of the gift of time and space for writing has been important, whether the gift was a room of one's own for a morning or a writer's retreat for a sabbatical season. What part has this sort of opportunity played for you?

AS: I grew up expecting what most women of my generation did. A woman became a nurse, schoolteacher or secretary. Then she married at 25 and let her husband support her. I stayed home a long time raising children. Before that, I was a secretary. I was always interested in going back to school, and I had always continued with my poetry to a certain extent. Yaddo was important because I had been a housewife for quite a while and it was good to get out of the house. Yaddo was an experience of freedom, time to think. It was shortly before I went back to the university. Maybe it was the first step toward that new freedom.

Going back to the university was important. It was a matter of finding something I could do that's worthwhile, that gave me a sense of ability. If I were to stay home and write, then I'd feel my primary duty might be to my family, but if I have a job that people respect, then if I stop that job, to write, it's an altogether different way of looking at my writing. It's not just taking time away from my family; it's a real choice then. The fact that you get money for your job is important—people recognize your ability with pay.

Question: What would you like to say when you're teaching? What would you most like your students to take away with them?

AS: I just think that people should like to learn and that learning should be something that is exciting and pleasant and worth doing. One can't always keep that posture in the classroom day after day, but learning is really a lot of fun and people ought to know that.

Question: You've given me a perfect cue—what are you going to learn about or do next?

AS: There are a lot of things I'd like to do. I have an idea for another anthology, and I'd like to do more translations, and maybe some essays on gardens. I'd like to try writing a novel. And more poetry, of course. It's a matter of finding time and then focusing on one project.

I often think of a motto by Francis Bacon—"All rising to a great place is by a winding stair." Not that you expect to get to a great place, it's just that so often you try something and it comes to nothing, apparently; then a long time afterwards something grows out of it in a completely surprising way. I like mottos. There's another motto in *The Descent* . . .

Question: "In the Black Forest, 2." May I quote it here?

> Gone, gone but over me still
> Broods the winged bird of their spirit
> Made of their living breath.
> It will last in their children forever.
>
> It covers the bleak sky, a fierce mother—
> And from the claws drift down ribbons
> Curving scrolls with their mottos
> Which say *Do what you can* and *Take heart*.

AS: If they were real scrolls, they would say something like "*Virtus et fortitudo*," "Courage and Endurance," but I put it in colloquial English, "Do what you can" and "Take heart." In a world that sometimes moves between beauty and terror or emptiness, it's something to hold onto.

BARBARA GLENN, like Ann Stanford, is a native of southern California and currently resides there. Presently she is completing a dissertation in American literature for Stanford University where, a few years ago, she was a Stegner Fellow in Poetry. Her poems have appeared in various journals, most recently in *The Greensboro Review* and *The Southern Review*.

Ann Stanford: Narrative Biography

Ann Stanford's parents came to southern California from Texas during the teens of the century and settled in the small town of La Habra, where the poet was born and spent most of her early years.

"My father worked for an oil company; mother taught school. Our town was surrounded by and interspersed with old walnut orchards and orange and lemon groves. At night from the hills to the south I could hear the chug of the pumps of the oil wells. To the north were hills given over to citrus and avocado orchards and a stream shaded by a grove of native oaks which made a pleasant goal for my hikes."

She wrote poems from an early age and at nearby Fullerton Union High School studied with two inspiring teachers, Grace Gray Miller and Marjorie French. At Stanford University she was included in a group of poets associated with Yvor Winters. Through Winters she met Alan Swallow, poetry editor of the *New Mexico Quarterly*, in which her early poems appeared. Swallow also published her first two books.

Having majored in pre-law at Stanford, with a year in the Law School, she became a legal secretary in Los Angeles and later worked in the office of the County Superintendent of Schools. In 1942 she married Ronald A. White, an architect. They had three daughters and a son. After a number of years as a housewife, she returned to the university—this time UCLA—for graduate study in journalism and English with an emphasis on early American literature. She joined the English faculty of California State University, Northridge, in 1962 and has taught there ever since. With her husband and son she lives on a brush-covered hillside above Beverly Hills.

In 1969 she received The Shelley Memorial Award, in 1972 The Award in Literature of the National Institute—American Academy of Arts and Letters, in 1974 a grant in poetry from the National Endowment for the Arts.

Her poetry has appeared in such journals as *The New Yorker*, *The Atlantic*, *The New Republic* and *The Southern Review*, and she has written essays on poets and poetry for a number of scholarly journals. She is vice-president for the West Coast of The Poetry Society of America and a member of the Advisory Board of the Wallace Stevens Society. She has served as a judge for a number of awards, including the James D. Phelan Award in Poetry, the Hopwood Awards at the University of Michigan, and the Bush Foundation Fellowships in Minnesota.

Her latest poetry books, *In Mediterranean Air*, *The Descent* and *The Weathercock*, were published by Viking. *In Mediterranean Air* (1977) received The DiCastagnola Award of The Poetry Society of America.

Cindy Bellinger

LOS ALAMOS, NEW MEXICO

Children and Other Reasons

I

can you imagine where my love goes
if it falls behind the horizon each time?
it falls into children.
I try not to tell you this
because you don't know how to hold babies
you don't know how they find breasts
you don't know how your first child can't be mine
the one you never see
the one you call one's enough.
would you let me lick this anger from your neck?

II

lying on the beach last Tuesday
I thought how little the king must be
who lives in drip castles
and how Daddy scooted little sailboats
over a globe on Columbus Day
explaining just one more way the ocean is
I remember how private everything felt in the sand
everything buried except my head
no one knew I wiggled my toes

and lying there
I wanted to inhale the whole ocean
and let you walk to the edge and let you look down
into all my arms rocking babies
all the babies that I've dreamed of, wanted
and sent there to wait
I wanted you to lean over, lift up the fringe around
my shawl
see their hands
see where I am when you're not looking

III

now I wear skirts
that know what my hips will hold
I wonder how much room I have; how much longer;
and if these wishes echo through my clean hips.

my body slipped down my mother's long arms
out through her fingers into my hands
and I dress like my mother
I eat   I cry   I sew like my mother
I cook and plant flowers ride swim and scream
I look like my mother
I am my mother.
She knew the name of every shell
and now I do
and she wanted children
and now I can.

She took me to Mexico once. To an orphanage. I
        was ten.
All the babies had colds and wore white cotton
        dresses.
I wanted them all. She told me, "Mothers have lots of
children here."
And I watched the way their hips moved down the
        cobbled
stone streets like large warm cradles.

hips.
places for small hands and feet.
I wear them like skirts.

IV

can you imagine the ocean still in my mouth
and me lying here watching you wonder

89

why there are children?

I don't want to put the ocean back

I want you to know about the full skirts
gathered around Mexican women and how their
    shawls are full
of breasts and children
and at night how they have more and keep them in
    shawls,
then carefully unwrap them

when the first coconuts fall, full of strong names

I want you to know that someday my hips
will break open like an orphanage
and children will crawl down my legs
out my skirt into places in my arms

I want you to know
my love for you and all the children
are in the same place
and without you I'll have the wrong baby

Naomi Rachel

HOLLYWOOD, CALIFORNIA

The Very Rose

in this city
there are

no fountains
at night

alone
i arrive at the airport

through the tunnel
you emerge

with the very rose
i picked to give you

already yellow
in your lapel

William Carlos Williams' Buddy

my father thought
himself

a buddy
of william carlos williams

though they never met
or ever even

were in the same
place at the same time

but nevertheless
my father claims him

a comrade
of reality

a professional man
in a lucrative line

so aware
of economic priority

what he wrote
in spare time

was his
own business

Adelaide Blomfield

ANCHORAGE, ALASKA

Attics

1. Lace, velvet, my grandmother's dresses hang
   in webs of silk threads like butterflies
   and moths. Ribboned boxes, old letters, lie
   in the poverty of all that sprang
   from want of love. Crumbs for the sibling mouse,
   the gleam of wood, sofas with split seams,
   return again as winter's short dreams
   to all the waiting rooms of this house.

   Old love, I hear you moving like a ghost
   through empty corridors, up walled stairs.
   Wormwood, lavender, camphor everywhere
   a door is opened, linger when it's closed.

   We'd love so poor we borrowed love to fill
   our lives and found them wanting still.

2. We enter each other as we enter
   closed houses, slowly at first,
   afraid of touch me, touch me, in covered
   furniture's thick dust. We rehearse
   our careful speech, each of us alone.
   Like dull phonograph needles seeking
   songs in scratched records, we only
   disturb the quiet of these antiques.

   Stiff with old lace, time covers the chairs,
   waits in a bed cold as ivory.
   Mirrors at the bottom of endless stairs
   multiply candles, breath burns bodies
   like snow. In the shadows of slow fires,
   we move in rooms with lights from other lovers.

3. Once there were stones in our pockets to hold
   us down. Now paper moth words try wings,
   their tissue bodies hold air. We bring,
   with little faith, gifts that bind. Cold,
   we turn from sun, move in unhappy shadows
   when all that's lovely in love is more true
   than stones or wings that fail us. We are too
   hard on each other. Not hurt enough, we borrow
   grief, divide our lives in little rooms.
   Like mad old women taking tea with cats,
   unbutton our gloves, take off our hats,
   pretend yesterday, when all the while we're doomed
   to love: the imperfectibility
   of lips, those met mismatched; our own frailty.

4. So cold the air freezes, dropping in scales
   to cover the snow. Now the sky is gone
   in smoke dissolving to smoke, trailing
   like a tired breathing. I have begun
   to pack, returning to leave. Books lean
   in emptied shelves, splayed open, boxes half
   filled with newspaper, old magazines
   saved too long—these the unplanned epitaphs.

   Your mouth, soft as a dog fetching fallen
   birds, covers mine, but there is a weariness
   now, a gentleness of habit. To recall
   spring is to remember that geese carry
   winter in their breasts. In the fogged breath
   of windows, we look forever north.

5. We fell like leaves in love, accountable
   to no one, and in a while regained
   ourselves. Now it all returns again.

The whole year remembers spring's pull.
Your face brought back is like rain, full
of ghosts that whisper at the window panes,
filter through crevices and remain
diffused in light, pale and mutable.

How slow now rises the wild moon when
what was summer returns to haunt me.
Love must be this then:
a moon when the moon has gone brilliantly;
a pillow of arms beneath heads,
bodies tired with desire, revisited.

Susan Griffin

BERKELEY, CALIFORNIA

Deer Skull

for Hallie

1.

I keep placing my hands over
my face, the finger tips just
resting on the place where I feel
my eyebrows and the fine end
of a bone. My eyes are covered
with the blood of my hands, my
palms hold
my jaws. I do this at dinner
my daughter says
Are you all right
and by a common miracle
when I smile
she knows I am.

2.

I ask her what she will do
after we eat. Sleep she
tells me. But I will clean
the deer skull, wash it.

3.

You gave me this skull in the woods
told me to bring it clean
and tell the story I had told you
before, about how the deer had
come to me, and I said I would.

4.

And I put this skull on an old
newspaper, pulled the lower part
of the jaws free, touched it first
carefully, as if it would fall apart
in my hands, the bone paper
thin, and then I saw I could
scrub, so brushed the surface with
steel and my fingers and more
and more this surface became
familiar to me.

5.

I wanted to see the lines of it
what it would be if it had been
polished by the wind, the water
and my hands this agent making
the skull more itself.
Slowly I was not afraid at all
and my fingers went into the deepest
holes of this thing, not afraid
for myself or it, feeling
suddenly as if my cleaning this
small fragment of earth away
from the crevices inside was
like loving.

6.

But it was when I touched the place
where the eyes were that I knew
this was the shell of the deer that had
lived here, this was this deer
and not this deer, her home and
now empty of her, but not
empty of her, I knew also, not
empty of her, as my hands
trembled.

7.

And in that instant remembered you
had been in that body of
that deer dying, what
does it feel like to be a deer
dying, the death consumes
you like birth, you are
nowhere else but in the center.

8.

Remembering those gentle deer
that watched me as I wept,
or the deer that leapt as if
out of my mind, when I saw
speaking there in that green place
the authority of the heart,
and the deer of the woods where
my feet stood stared at me until
I whispered to her and cried
at her presence.

9.

And when I cleaned the skull
I washed myself and sat
my body half out of the water
and put my hands again over
my face, my fingers edging the
bone over my eyes, and I thought
how good this feels and this
is a gesture you make.

10.

Tell this story of the deer's skull
you asked gently and so I
came in my own time to put
these words carefully here
slowly listing each motion
on this thin paper
as fragile and as tough
as knowledge.

Tess Gallagher

TUCSON, ARIZONA

Painted Steps

I was coming down the wide, painted steps.
I wanted to go with you
in your leaving, the way a farmer would go
behind his horse
to keep the rows straight. Even
when we reached the car door and I knew
the field would not get there in time,
I thought surely he'll find a way
to walk from this so I can see him harmed
and unsure like a man
who would turn back if
he could, if the field were not coming
late under its flock of birds.

The last moments when you leaned
from the car, even then
I thought if only we could believe this
as never, the field would have mercy, would
come down around us like a fine, healing
rain. I stood where the car had been
and looked out as far as I could, believing
so the light would deepen
and drop off, the field
empty and settle one patch of sky.
But no, I'm not one of those
who changes an ending to keep the moment true.
Think of me as one who lives things quickly,
cruelly as a car could live it.
Think of me as one who stands in the streets,
speeding past with the stopped wheel
in my hands, and the radio, its
small hearth flickering
along the trees ahead.

In That Time When It Was Not the Fashion

When the daughters came for me
with their hands webbed in each other's hair,
when they saw, even to the last, how desire
kept me ripe, they grew tender
as the portraits of swans
whose necks are threaded on the open
pond. Their arms at my waist
were strong, were yearning.

We walked near the water's edge.
I told them the one story I called
my life as it began
when I looked back in that far place.

On the table in the land of hunters
I said, there was meat
and it was eaten. I was born there
with brothers. They learned the ways
of the fathers, could take animals
unawares. Some with their bows
left many days and came to the fire
miraculous, the white deer
on their arrows carrying them far
into pardon. Others returned the same day
and leaned their guns
in the doorway. They were not deceived
about death. The elk hung
their golden heads in the dirt
of the shed. A long suddenness had
closed their eyes open. I
was a child with other children. We

crept up. Our house
had been blessed. We touched
the cold fur, the bald eyes.

My teeth were sharp. I could see the shape
of a leaf in the dark. In one bed
we slept and in the night
we held each other without words or
desire, my brothers now with wives.
Nearest blood that they were, my
changes drove them from me.
My hair was a veil at my back to catch
what looks would follow.

A tall man came into my life. He
liked to dance and be sung to. "Bend
to me," I said, "but not
too far. I like
to reach up." In a time
when it was not fashionable, I neglected
every good chance to live for myself
alone. "What
do you need?" I said. "What pleases

you?" Even to those unfaithful,
at some ripe moment, I could refuse them
nothing. I sent letters
absolving what hurt they might fear
to have done me. I pledged, I
said, "You are remembered well."
When they brought their new, their old
loves to meet me, I embraced them, I
let my picture be taken in their company.
I learned, in short, to stand with them
in the beloved past moments
so that nothing might be lost.

I would give you hope
against all this if I could.
But I cannot. I have drunk insects
at night from the river. Nor
did I wait for the fruit to fall.
I walked without thinking who lives
in the ground, too many steps. Not even
my death will have me. I am old
and unfinished. Keep watch for me.
I will have children to give away.

Contributors' Notes

Mary Barnard, when young, sent poems to Pound, beginning a life-long correspondence. Pound suggested she study Sapphic meter, a study which led to her *Sappho: A New Translation*. Even some twenty years after publication, this is the tenth position best seller on the University of California paperback list. Her *The Collected Poems* (Breitenbush) is due out this fall.

Cindy Bellinger, in 1978, taught for a bilingual-bicultural Colorado program; now in New Mexico, she is becoming a midwife and, also, is giving journal writing workshops in Los Alamos and Santa Fe. She says that she and her six-toed cat enjoy being members of New Mexico's active creative community. Willow Tree published her *Animal Again* and *Signatures*.

Adelaide Blomfield co-edits *Raven Magazine*. She has two books, *White Ash* (Charas Press) and *The Sound of Breathing* (Solo Press). Her recent book manuscript is of sonnets, some of which appear in this issue. Besides wearing her hats of writer and publisher, she wears other hats of poetry administrator, teacher, and active businesswoman.

Olga Broumas, a 1978 NEA recipient, spent six months writing, 11 months revising, the poetry sequence which appears in this issue. Born in Syros, Greece, in 1949, she has been a waitress and a barber, an instructor in modern dance and in modern and classic Greek, and is always a poet. Her fourth book, *Soie Sauvage* (Copper Canyon Press), is due out soon.

Mary Crow received the NEH research fellow $15,000 stipend for 1978–79. With this grant, she completed articles on, and translated, important Latin American surrealist works. Last spring, she won the 1979 Translation Award from Columbia University. *Border* (Boa Press), her first full length book of poems, is forthcoming.

Elaine Dallman, in the traditional manner, married and raised children; only afterwards, while learning what poetry is, did she recognize her talent and need for poetry. Her work has been the subject of a paper at the MLA and, in 1978, of articles in *La Isha* (Tel Aviv) and *Itinerary 7*. Concerned both for poetry and for women, wherever she lives, she activates women's studies.

Joanne de Longchamps demonstrates her dual abilities as a poet and as an artist known for collages in her sixth book, *The One Creature* (West Coast Poetry Review). Publication of this collection of twenty earlier poems and ten full-color collages was supported by the Nevada State Council on the Arts.

Kathleen Fraser has read poetry to campus audiences as widely separated as Harvard and Berkeley, Minnesota and San Diego. She conceived of the American Poetry Archive Videotape Library, organized it and directed it for three years. Also, she has been director of the Poetry Center, San Francisco State University. Of her six books of poetry, her most recent is *New Shoes* (Harper & Row).

Tess Gallagher, aided by a Guggenheim, spent some of '78 writing poetry full time, isolated in a house on the beach by Port Townsend. Then she taught in Texas and, next, traveled to Mexico. Last fall she moved to Arizona, to teach. Her first book, *Instructions to the Double* (Graywolf), is a recent winner of the Elliston Award. Her second book, *Under Stars* (Graywolf), came out in '78.

Sandra M. Gilbert was one of the 1978 winners of the Associated Writing Programs book manuscript contest. That collection, *In the Fourth World* (Alabama Press), was out early in 1979. Among recent critical publications, she has co-edited *Shakespeare's Sisters*, an anthology of essays on woman poets, and co-authored a book on nineteenth-century literary imagination.

Rita Garitano has worked for the Arizona Arts Commission's Poets-on-the-Road program for the past six years. She is also a featured face, photographically, in *The Face of Poetry* (La Verne Clark). Her recent poems have appeared in *New Mexico Magazine*, *Isthmus*, and others. Her first book of poems is *We Do What We Can* (Desert First Works).

Joy Harjo received an NEA Fellowship in 1978. She presently teaches creative writing at the Institute of American Indian Arts, an all-Indian junior college in Santa Fe. Her work has appeared in magazines such as *The New America*, *Yardbird*, and others. *What Moon Drove Me to This* (Reed and Cannon) is her latest book.

Patricia Henley, most recently, taught poetry to alcoholics and drug addicts at a residential treatment center. She has worked for six years in Poets-in-the-Schools programs in South Carolina, Georgia, Washington and Oregon. *Learning to Die* (Three Rivers Press) is her recent first book.

Suzanne Juhasz has had her poetry published by many journals and anthologies. *A Romance* (Out of Sight Press) came out in 1979. Her books of criticism are *Naked and Fiery Forms: Modern American Poetry by Women, A New Tradition*, and *Metaphor and the Poetry of Williams, Pound and Stevens*. She is presently at work on a novel and a book on Emily Dickinson.

Phyllis Koestenbaum, after not writing for 25 years, returned to the writing of poetry three years ago. Before, she had studied with John Ciardi, Theodore Morrison, Richard Wilbur and Archibald MacLeish. Last year she studied with William Dickey. Her first full-length book of poems, *oh I can't she says* (Christopher's) is due out in spring 1980.

Joan LaBombard describes her husband as her "grant-in-aid" for her many creative works. She first published in 1950, most recently in *The Nation* and *Prairie Schooner*. Many of her poems have been reprinted in the Borestone Mountain Poetry Awards anthologies. In 1979 she received the Consuela Ford Award, her fifth major award from the Poetry Society of America.

Adrianne Marcus has two hobbies, sub-atomic physics and reading; she recognizes one holiday, Halloween. Passage of Proposition 13 coincided with a decision to leave teaching to earn her living writing. *The Chocolate Bible*, an encyclopedia, came out in spring '79. Her third book of poetry, *Child of Earthquake Country* (New World Press) is due out soon.

Colleen J. McElroy received the Pushcart Prize for poetry in 1976 and an NEA Fellowship in 1978. *Music from Home: Selected Poems* came out in 1976. Her third book, *Winters without Snow* (Copper Canyon) presently is in galleys. She has recently published in *Poetry Northwest, The Chowder Review, 13th Moon, Seneca Review*, and others.

Rosalie Moore, with a poet's ability to turn material from musty archives into a freshly told story, wrote *Year of the Children*, a combination of unusual narrative and lyrical poems nominated for the Pulitzer award. She has received two Guggenheims in her well-published career. *Of Singles and Doubles* (Woolmer/Brotherson) was her '79 book.

Sheila Bunker Nickerson, named Poet Laureate of Alaska, where she has lived for seven years, has a new book of poetry, *Songs of the Pine-Wife* (Copper Canyon Press). In three earlier books, from Thorp Springs Press (two of poetry and one a novel), she uses details from her Alaskan environment as metaphors. She has won the Pushcart and Borestone poetry awards.

Diana Ó Hehir has been writing poetry only for the last six years, and has "been marvelously helped by other poets and by perceptive editors." Her poetry has brought her many successes, including the Devins Award for her first book, *Summoned* (University of Missouri Press), and publication of her second collection, *The Power to Change Geography* (Princeton University Press), in spring 1979.

Naomi Rachel has over 100 poems published in the United States and Canada, in anthologies and quarterlies such as *Hawaii Review, Contemporary California Poets, Malahat Review, Women of the Future, Aphra*. She spent last year teaching as the visiting poet at the University of British Columbia.

Adrien Stoutenburg authors prose and poetry books for young readers, with some thirty-five published. Of her adult poetry books, *Heroes, Advise Us* (Scribner) won the Lamont Award for the best first poetry book in 1964; *Short History of the Fur Trade* (Houghton Mifflin) came out in 1970; *Greenwich Mean Time* (University of Utah Press) came out fall 1979.

Phyllis Hoge Thompson is Director of Creative Writing at the University of Hawaii. In 1966 she invented *Haku Mele*, a Poets-in-the-Schools Program in Hawaii, one of the earliest in the nation. Her third poetry book is *The Serpent of the White Rose*. Currently, she is writing a long poem based on Hawaiian mythological material.

Chocolate Waters has performed over fifty poetry readings at universities, coffeehouses, local theatres, and on the radio. Her work appears frequently in women's publications such as *Moving Out, off our backs, Big Mama Rag*. Her books are *To the Man Reporter from the Denver Post* and *Take Me Like a Photograph*, both by Eggplant Press.

Kathleene West stayed on to work with Copper Canyon Press as a printer and book designer after completing their apprenticeship program. They printed her recent poetry book, *Land Bound*; Seal Press printed her 1978 fiction book. She has read widely throughout the Puget Sound area, and in Seattle, a few years ago, she was named an Artist of the City.

Gift Subscriptions

☐ Please enter a gift subscription for:

Recipient _____

Address _____

City _____ State _____ Zip _____

Recipient _____

Address _____

City _____ State _____ Zip _____

Recipient _____

Address _____

City _____ State _____ Zip _____

Gift Subscriptions

Recipients will be sent a gift announcement in your name; subscriptions begin with the present volume (*The West*).

Collectors' Copies: Hard Cover Limited Editions: $12.95 plus $1.00 handling.
Soft Cover Regular Editions, Individuals $6.00 each plus 50¢ handling, Institutions $9.00 each.

One year rates, (two volumes, *The West* and *The Northeast*):
Individuals $10.00, Students $9.00, Institutions $16.00.
(*Countries other than U.S. add $2.00 postage.*)

Two year rates (complete set of four regional volumes, beginning with this inaugural volume):
Individuals $18.00, Students $16.00, Institutions $28.00.
(*Countries other than U.S. add $3.00 postage.*)

☐ Please enter a gift subscription at the rate circled above for the recipient(s).

☐ Please enter my subscription at the rate circled above.

Total enclosed: $ _____ Date: _____

Name _____

Address _____

_____

City _____ State _____ Zip _____

Mail with your check or purchase order to *Woman Poet*, Women-in-Literature, Incorporated, P.O. Box 12668, Reno, Nevada, 89510.

DATE DUE

JUL 1 1984			
MAY 2 8 1988			
JUN 2 5 1990			
OCT 2 1 1990			

PRINTED IN U.S.A.

HIGHSMITH 45-102